The Cowboy and His Interpreters

"A COWBOY IS A MAN WITH GUTS AND A HORSE."

The Cowboy and His Interpreters

Douglas Branch

Illustrations by
Will James
Joe de Yong
Charles M. Russell

Introduction by
Harry Sinclair Drago

COOPER SQUARE PUBLISHERS, INC.
59 Fourth Avenue, New York 3, N. Y.

Library of Congress Catalog Card Number: 62-7732

59 Fourth Avenue, New York 3, N. Y.

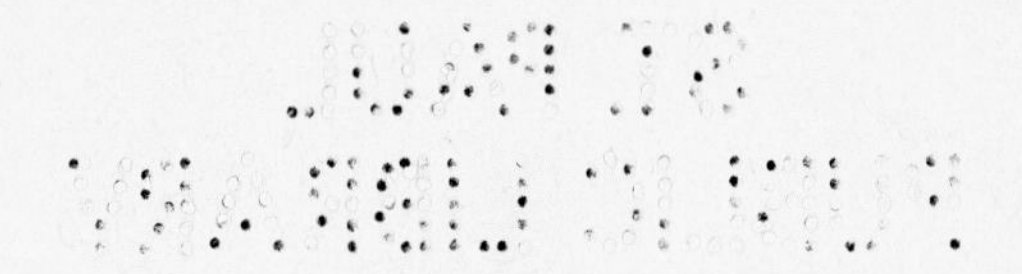

DEDICATED TO
THE OLD-TIME TRAIL DRIVERS OF TEXAS
WITH A BOW TO
LOUIS PELZER

CONTENTS

ILLUSTRATIONS

ILLUSTRATIONS

INTRODUCTION

Not long ago I had occasion to climb the narrow iron stairway that leads to the balcony above the south General Reading Room of the New York Public Library, where the many heavy volumes of the exhaustive catalog of the Library of Congress is to be found.

I had never been there before, and not expecting to be there soon again, my embarrassing ego prompted me, after I had found the information I wanted, to see what this greatest of all book catalogs had to say about me. What I found was staggering. There in black ink I stood undressed for all the world to see, at least the infinitesimal part of it that might be interested. The compilers had stripped me to the skin, revealing the titles published over my own name, my pen names and the books written with this or that collaborator. There was page after page of it.

Almost without exception they are books, fiction and non-fiction, dealing with the American West. Based on that accumulated evidence, I do not think anyone easily could deny me the right to express my opinion of and enthusiasm for the reappearance, after many years of being unavailable, of Douglas Branch's *The Cowboy and His Interpreters.*

A lot of water has gone over the dam since it was originally published in 1926. That was the year I first went to Hollywood, back in the days of the silent motion pictures, to write for Tom Mix, the "cowboy" star. The reviews of Branch's book were excellent, and I bought it and read it with solid satisfaction; it seemed to say what I had been trying to say for four years. It was a book that Hollywood writers and directors sorely needed; but they didn't buy it; they were making a "product," labelled Western, though there was very little of the real West about it, other than horses and scenery. Even the so-called "cowboy" stars were, with one exception, synthetic. The garb they wore would have shamed to death any old-time, honest-to-God cowpuncher caught wearing such attire.

As Branch observes, the Western motion-picture was trash, acknowledged as such by the producer, made according to a long established formula and outrageously profitable. It could be, and was, made over and over with only a change of place and character names and a new feminine interest for the star. It was self-perpetuating, and what we have on Western television shows today is its shoddy but legitimate offspring. Its plot, characters and wanton disregard for anything approaching historical fidelity are the same.

When Douglas Branch put his book together the movies had not yet learned how to talk and television was still in the somewhat distant future. Judging by his penetrating and caustic appraisal of what had been offered in the past as so-called "Western" sagas and epics, it seems safe to believe that he would have looked aghast at the "Western" saturation of the air by the latest and greatest of all mass media. I should like to think that he would feel as I do about television's twisting and outrageous disregard of historical fact and its libeling of the West by plucking known scoundrels out of the past and transforming them into heroic champions of law and order.

In 1922, four years prior to the appearance of *The Cowboy and His Interpreters,* Philip Ashton Rollins, in his *The Cowboy,* made the first serious attempt to reveal the fictional image of the cowboy, which the public had accepted as genuine, for the absurd caricature it was, and depict the rarely picturesque, usually shabby, unlettered, loyal, hard-riding, tireless and fearless cowpuncher as he really was.

You will find it listed as preferred reading in the bibliographies of half a hundred books concerned with the Western scene. It is a respected book and has long since been a collector's item. The same can be said for Douglas Branch's *The Cowboy and His Interpreters.* It too was a "first," with its history of the evolution of the Western story from the days of the Alkali Ike era and the Dime Novel to Owen Wister, who made the Western novel respectable with *The Virginian.* Wister opened the door for the immensely successful historical romances of Emerson Hough, *The Covered Wagon, Fifty-four Forty or Fight,*

North of 36, and enabled Eugene Manlove Rhodes, the cowboy turned author, and considered by many to have been the most literate of all cowboy interpreters (an opinion which I share), to find a devoted and critical audience. Best of all, Western *aficionados* turned back to the forgotten books of Andy Adams, the Texan, which, though they lacked literary polish had the vitality, saltiness, and flavor of reality possible only in a writer who knows what he is writing about.

I came along a little too late to merit Branch's attention, but I was fortunate enough in later years to become personally acquainted with most of the men and women whose work he evaluates. I find myself disagreeing with some of his judgments. I believe he was too lavish in his praise in some instances and too niggardly in others. By any yardstick you care to apply, Alexander Wasson and Caroline Lockhart deserve to be listed among the top practitioners in the field of the Western novel. Branch does not mention them. There may be others. But he was doing something that had not been done before. If he missed one or two of the greats or near-greats of their time, it is understandable.

Wister's *The Virginian* had a subtitle: *A Horseman of the Plains,* which few remember. It was sold as *A Romance of Cattleland.* Douglas Branch was the first and I believe the only critic to point out that there are no cattle in the story. It is a criticism that can be leveled at fifty per cent of the so-called "cowboy-cattle" novels. This is a shortcoming hardly due to accident; too many writers who found writing the Western story lucrative employment knew little or nothing about working cattle, and therefore concealed their ignorance by avoiding the subject, though it was around cattle that the rangeland story revolved.

The Western story has been called "the hardiest weed that ever grew on the literary landscape." It has been abused, caricatured, lampooned, ridiculed and cheapened, but it has survived. It also has been called America's one truly indiginous folk tale, unrelated to any other country. At its best it can be and often is literature; at its worst it is trash.

The Dime Novel left no permanent mark on the reading habits of the nation. The stream of yarns turned out by Ned Buntline and a host of imitators were too outrageously incredible to be taken seriously by any but adolescents. They grew up and forgot about them. It was the pulp magazine, as Branch observes, that fashioned a trend and put its indelible mark on the Western story. In the twenty-odd years in which the Western pulps flourished and made fortunes for their publishers, only three editors bucked the tide of banality and mediocrity that surrounded them and demanded material turned out by competent, professional writers. There was Bob Davis, of *Argosy*, the best fiction editor we ever produced; Arthur Sullivant Hoffman, of *Adventure Magazine*, and Harry Maule, editor of the Doubleday Westerns, Short Stories, West and Frontier. The rest were, with one or two exceptions, just hatchet men, wedded to the formula that said if one thrill in a story was good, two were twice as good, and so on up until the accumulated thrills thrilled no one, and the pulps declined.

It has been said that the paperbacks put the pulps out of business. That is not true; the Western pulps were on their way to oblivion before the paperbacks gained their phenomenal popularity.

Branch remarks about the care the working cowboy took of his hands; that he often wore gloves as protection against rope burns, which could keep a man useless for a week to ten days. Because his hands were so important to him in his work, he didn't indulge in fist-fighting; he held fist-fighting to be a cut beneath him, something good enough for soldiers and mule skinners but not for him. And yet the fist fight and the six-gun are the basic props of every Western television show you see.

It was the editors of the pulps who put the fist fight into the Western story — one man in particular; I could name him. His theory ran this way: if the first clash between the good guys and the bad guys went as far as gunfire, somebody had to be shot; if the hero always escaped unmarked, plausibility suffered; if he was wounded (the shoulder was always a good place) he was on the shelf a few days, never a good place for a hero to be. By substituting fists for guns in the first clash, you could keep the big gun battle for the climax of the story. In short order every pulp on the market adopted that format. It increased suspense, added to the urgency of the story and presented the opportunity for more and more action. Since action is the backbone of the Western television show, it quite naturally purloined the idea, there being no surer way to get action than through violence, and the fist fight has become as sadistic, furniture-breaking, blood-letting and almost as satisfying to the customers as the bark of a six-gun.

I wish Branch had seen fit to include a chapter on Western art, particularly in the field of depicting the old-time puncher and the Texas pony. Every phase of those old days and old-timers has been captured and put on paper or canvas by such men as Charles M. Russell, Frederic Remington, Frank Tenney Johnson, Joe DeYoung, Ross Santee, Will James and a score more. Their pictures always tell a story, one that is understandable at a glance, like the postcard-size painting Charlie Russell sent his boss in Helena during the winter of '87, the year of the big die-up, when eighty per cent of the range cattle in Eastern Montana froze or starved to death, showing an old skin and bones Longhorn steer standing in the snow, on his last legs, surrounded by a ring of wolves. Across the bottom of the card Charlie wrote, "The Last of Five Thousand." A thousand words could not have told the story better or more completely.

We have some excellent cowboy verse. Branch pays tribute to Henry Herbert Knibbs. And there is Omar Barker, who rates with the best. I can close my eyes now and hear Gene Rhodes reciting Knibbs with moving nostalgia and affection: "Morning on the Malibu where once we used to ride . . ."

John A. Lomax had published his collection of old cowboy songs. Many of them are widely known today. Douglas Branch was one of the first to recognize the importance of the contribution Professor Lomax had made to our understanding of the cowboy. The verses themselves seldom rise above doggeral, and the tunes are hardly music, but if you ever listened to the night chants of cowboys guarding a herd, you know there was magic in it.

The West that was is getting farther away from us year after year, but thanks to careful and diligent research by dedicated historians we know more about it today than we did back in the '20's. Branch made good use of the avenues of information open to him. Obviously, microfilm and tape recordings were not available, and such citadels of information as the Oklahoma Historical Society and the Kansas State Historical Society, to name just two, possessed few of the facilities that the writer enjoys today.

Quite naturally Branch committed some errors. None are of such great consequence that they cannot be forgiven.

He goes astray in locating the Chisholm Trail and giving its position relative to the much older Shawnee Trail. He says: "The Old Shawnee Trail, after running parallel to the Chisholm Trail for about a hundred miles, veered to the west to strike Baxter Springs in Kansas. The West Chisholm Trail, to avoid later settlements, penetrated into western Kansas to Ellsworth."

He is badly mistaken in this instance. The Old Shawnee Trail, entering Indian Territory from the southeast about where Fort Gibson was located, went up the Grand River for some miles, and after crossing to the east bank of the river pointed into southwestern Missouri, in the white man's time to Sedalia. In fact, it was often called the Sedalia Trail. The warlike Osage Nation pushed the Shawnees into the discard and the old trail became the principal avenue for their scalp and horse-stealing forays into Texas. The old trail acquired a new name, the Osage Trace, and it in time gave way to still a third name, the Texas Road.

The Texas Road first crossed Red River at Rock Bluff Crossing, and a few years later down the river a short distance at Colbert's Ferry, one of the three great cattle crossings of the Big Red. The big herds going up the Chisholm Trail crossed at Red River Station, a hundred and twenty-five miles to the west.

Branch further confuses the matter by mentioning a West Chisholm Trail. I can only say on unimpeachable authority that there never was a West Chisholm Trail. The only explanation I can give is that he gave the name to an east-west trail running from Fort Gibson to Chisholm's trading post on the North Canadian, and on the early Government maps given as "Chisholm's Cattle Trail." It was not part of the famous trail that, according to some, began down around San Antonio and ran all the way up to Abilene, Kansas. The only segment of it that Jesse Chisholm pioneered was the wagon road from his ranch on the Little Arkansas to the new Wichita Agency on the Washita River, a distance of 200 miles.

Speaking of the great cattle drives, Branch

says: "The northern drives became established as an institution in 1867, when Abilene, on the Kansas Pacific Railroad . . . despatched press-agents south to urge the advantages of taking herds to Abilene." The facts do not bear him out. Joseph G. McCoy, the founder of the Texas Cattle Trade, sent two agents into Texas to drum up business; not the railroad company. In fact, the Kansas Pacific had no faith in the success of the market, did nothing for McCoy and even refused to honor its contracts with him when payment came due. Branch is also in error when he says the end of the great cattle drives was "foreshadowed in 1880 by the closure of the Chisholm trail." It was not until after 1885 that the Chisholm Trail was abandoned, and the drives shifted to the new Western Trail to Dodge City, crossing Red River at Doan's Store. He does not mention the Western Trail by that name but calls it the Texas Trail. A few Texans so identified it, but it was as the Western Trail, coming north by way of Fort Griffen, passing through the Wichita Mountains to Mobeetie and Longhorn Crossing on the Cimarron that it appears in history.

It may seem to be splitting hairs to point out to the reader that barbed wire did not arrive in Texas in 1873, as the author says. Barbed wire was not put on the market until 1875.

These are errors that I am sure Douglas Branch would have corrected had he been given the opportunity to do so. He was too thorough and conscientious a writer not to have done so. Having made some errors of my own, through carelessness and misinformation, I know they distress the author far more than the reader.

Harry Sinclair Drago

June 24th, 1961

The Cowboy and His Interpreters

" 'Tain't often we git together
To swap yarns an' tell our lies,"
Said the old time Texas cowman
As a mist comes to his eyes.
"So let's drink up; here's how!"
As we drain our glasses two,
"Them was good ol' days an' good ol' ways—
Now I'm tellin' you!"

OLD SONG.

THE COWBOY AND HIS INTERPRETERS

CHAPTER ONE

TEXAS CATTLE AND TEXAS COWBOYS

THE sun-god Osiris was represented in the Egyptian zodiac, in delicate compliment, as a bull; and the great landowners of the fifth and sixth dynasties listed herds of cattle high among their possessions. In the Delta and elsewhere the "open range" prevailed; cattle wandered where they would, each carrying on its shoulder the brand of its owner. The "rustler" was an institution of the cattle-country then as later; the ranchmen of the Delta were notoriously apt at incorporating into their own herds cattle that had drifted north into the lowlands. The cowboys must have roped and branded with a litheness that the art of the Theban tomb paintings does not admit; but the gusto, the intoxication with life, of the American cowboy of the open ranges of our West could not have been shared by them.

There must have been no Egyptian equivalent to

Come all you jolly cowboys that follow the broncho steer,
I'll sing to you a verse or two your spirits for to cheer,

nor to such a pleasant tribute to the home ranch as

You work hard all day and come in at night,
And turn your horse loose, for they say it's all right,
And set down to supper and begin to complain
Of the chuck that you get on the U-S-U range.

The Egyptian cowboy was a cowboy by occupation, not a cowboy by calling; for Egypt was a Servile State. Texas—once a Republic, always a name to be apostrophized in ballads and drunk down in whisky, mescal, or Clicquot Club—was the real birthplace of the cowboy as one more than a workman, one with a tradition and a psychology of his own, a figure destined to become a literary tradition.

The Mexican herder, the *vaquero,* became a fixture soon after the Spaniards brought cattle and horses from Spain. According to the tradition of the range, Cortez had a brand in the form of three Christian crosses, the first brand to be used on the North American continent. These original herds increased rapidly, and scores of long-horned, wild cattle, finding gradually a wider range to the northward, advanced in time across the Rio Grande. Some of these cattle that reached Texas were fugitives from the herds in old Mexico; others were under the control of *vaqueros* whose rifles held the range against the Indians.

The history of the American cowboy does not begin with a simple displacement of the Mexican, with methods and customs in handling cattle waiting only to be appropriated. Mexican temperament had been easily contented. The Abbé Domenech wrote of the Mexican cattlemen: "When the ranchero is not either resting or amusing himself, he mounts his horse and canters over the plains and through the woods to see his herds, to visit his friends, to buy provisions, or assist at a feast, a baptism, a marriage, or join in the fandango, but the ranchero never walks. . . . He is content with a wretched hut for his residence, while he decorates his saddle and bridle with gold and silver ornaments. At home he is all filth; mounted on his horse he wears the gayest attire." Occasionally he visited his stock, "perhaps to know what horses might be sold at the next fair . . . or to mark the oxen to be killed for his *tassejo*"—his "jerked beef." The peon that attended to the herding was no more an approximation of the American cowboy than his master was an approximation of the American ranch-owner; and under his desultory care much of the Spanish stock escaped, to mix with the cattle that the American colonists in Texas had brought with them from the States. The Texas Longhorn, the staple of the early Western cattle trade, was in consequence a slight modification for the better of the thin-legged, wiry Spanish stock.

Young Texans whose taste for fast riding and an exciting life had only been whetted by the Texan Revolution turned naturally from pursuing fugitive Mexicans and hunting down Indians to gathering wild cattle and driving them eastward to market or to keep.

The Mexican rancheros had migrated beyond the Rio Grande in the stress of the Revolution; the Indians had destroyed their buildings; but there remained many thousands of cattle that had lapsed into wildness. "The first cowboys," mostly young men from the Nueces region that had won notice for their hard riding and accurate shooting, found Mex-

MEXICAN VAQUERO—ROPING

ican *vaqueros* to tutor them in the handling of these cattle, and became young capitalists—but capitalists without a market. If the cattle were to be handled for profit, men willing to undertake the hazards of long drives into country of which the *vaqueros* had heard many fearful stories had to supplant the Mexican herders.

Drives were made to New Orleans, the metropolis of the Gulf country, in 1842 and in after years; but that city could obtain near at hand all the cattle it needed. As long as Texas cattle could only be slaughtered for their hides and tallow, nearly all of the work was done by Mexicans. The demand of the Forty-Niners in California for food supplies induced some Texas stockmen to attempt the long drive of at least fifteen hundred miles into an unknown country, and for a short while the high prices justified braving the dangers and the great loss of cattle on the trail; the real importance of the movement was its bringing Americans into the places which only Mexicans had held. Drives into Mexico were also attempted, but they found little market and small profit.

The attempt of one James Foster to build up a business of sending steers to New Orleans by steamship, an enterprise which introduced big-business methods to the Texans when Foster acquired a monopoly of the carrying trade, provided an interlude. In 1846 Edward Piper drove a thousand Texas cattle to Ohio, where they were fattened and sold. Ten years later drives were made to St. Louis; the drovers realized a moderate profit, and were encouraged to follow the trail in the next year. These pioneer drives continued until the Civil War. Then the cattlemen and cowboys of Texas left for the service; and the cattle, over three million of them, were left to drift at will.

Those ranchmen that returned to Texas after the War found their cattle scattered over the plains, in the brush, in the coulees. The Confederate authorities had taken many of them, leaving the cattlemen to bear the loss as "a contribution to the cause." Indians had raided the herds, and renegades had come back to brand the cattle for themselves. The number of unbranded cattle on the range, the increase of the years of war that had survived the drouth of almost three years, invited the young man returning from war to enter the field as though he were a legitimate stock-owner, and brand as large a herd as his inclination and energies suggested. This easy assumption of ownership doubtless had much to do in establishing the peculiar Texas morality that Scotch and Yankee cattle-magnates in a later era found very distressing. In 1886 Charlie Siringo, covetous of great riches, harkened back to those days when, if he had taken time by the forelock, he might have been wallowing in wealth with the rest of the cattle kings—"or to use a more appropriate name," he added in malicious humor, "cattle thieves." But alas, he thought, "the days of honorable cattle stealing is past, and I must turn my mind into a healthier channel." So Charlie Siringo wrote a book for butcher-boys to sell in smoking-cars.

The trail to the north reopened after the War, and Texas cattle at last had a steady market.

The greatest of these trails was the Chisholm trail, named from the half-breed Indian, Jesse Chisholm, who, the cowboys agreed, was the first man to drive a herd northward into Kansas through the Indian lands in the present Oklahoma. In the spring of 1865 Jesse Chisholm had set out from his temporary home near the mouth of the Little Arkansas River, on a trading trip to the valleys of the Canadian and Washita Rivers, in the Indian Territory. He led his wagon-train over the faint trace of the trail made four years before by the Federal troops under Colonel Emory, when they had withdrawn from posts in the Indian Territory and marched to Fort Leavenworth with Captain Black Beaver of the Delaware tribe as their guide. This trail was picked by the cattlemen as they crossed their herds over the Red River, and became known as the Chisholm trail. But in a few years the making of the Chisholm trail had become flowered by legend, until few were sure where the trail began and how it had been first traced.

The Old Shawnee trail, after running parallel to the Chisholm trail for about a hundred miles, veered to the west to strike Baxter Springs in Kansas. The West Chisholm trail, to avoid later settlements, penetrated into western Kansas to Ellsworth. To the west was the Pecos trail, with paths from the west and southwest converging at Horsehead Crossing on the Pecos River; and between this and the Chisholm trail, to name only one other, was the Panhandle trail, perhaps the hardest of the drives, touching the unwatered table-lands of the Llano Estacado, the Staked Plains, a route traveled by thousands of cattle into Colorado and western Kansas.

In a "fenceless empire" of open, unclaimed lands, there was much branching out and interweaving of minor trails into these great pathways. Yet custom and distances dictated a certain conformity, and the Chisholm trail in the seventies was trampled and torn down by thousands of hoofs until it became "a chocolate band amid the green prairies," flanked by little banks of sand and studded by the bleaching skeletons of cattle and horses. Up the Chisholm trail came Texas cowboys, following a route that brought them into new country, and leaving it where they might taste new pleasures and then return to await the drives of the next year, or stay in the north for work on the range that stretched from the edge of the farmer's settlements to the Rockies—the new cattle-country that was opened up with the coming of cattle from Texas and the invasion of the West by the railroads. When Wyoming and Montana, in the late seventies and early eighties, imported great herds of cattle from Texas, Texas cowboys came with them. Young men from the East and the Middle West attracted to this wild life on the plains, about which a tradition was already forming, found Texans bossing them and Texans working with them. And the Texan, proud of his priority, and delighting in the glamour of his early life, took the ambitious newcomer in hand, and tutored him in range customs and range lore. "Very many respectable young men were carried away under those subtle influences," wrote a Scotchman distressed at the ways of these reckless fellows. "Their morals were corrupted."

The thin-lipped Middle West, as yet virginal of the urge to sow its own wild oats, did not know what to make of the exuberant, easy-going Texan; and as the "natives" observed that saloons increased as the number of Texas cowboys increased, and cattle-rustling seemed to grow similarly, decided he must be an inferior sort of person. The editor of the Topeka Commonwealth, in his issue for August 15, 1871, passed judgment for his fellow-Kansans: "The Texas cattle herder is a character, the like of which can be found nowhere else on earth. Of course he is unlearned and illiterate, with but few wants and meager ambition. His diet is principally navy plug and whisky and the occupation dearest to his heart is gambling. His dress consists of a flannel shirt with a handkerchief encircling his neck, butternut pants and a pair of long boots, in which are always the legs of his pants. His head is covered by a sombrero, which is a Mexican hat with a high crown and a brim of enormous dimensions. He generally wears a revolver on each side of his person, which he will use with as little hesitation on a man as on a wild animal. Such a character is dangerous and desperate and each one has generally killed his man." The gentleman concludes: "They drink, swear, and fight, and life with them is a round of boisterous gayety and indulgence in sensual pleasure."

On his native range the dangers of the frontier and the fiery temper of the Longhorns, the incessant alertness for traces of Indians and the dexterity needed to handle the Texas steer, were the forces that molded the Texas cowboy.

The Longhorn cattle were half-wild beasts, unmodified by the Shorthorn strains that came into the northern ranges from the east, and steeped in malevolent cleverness accumulated through years of vigilant freedom. The Texan loved these cattle because they fought him. "There were times when the steer would get spooky and mad, and wouldn't turn even if you'd fan him acrost the face with your rope, sometimes that fanning would get him on the 'prod' . . . and then them long horns of his would get mighty dangerous to man and horse, but the *cowboy* never lets a critter get away."

Decoys were often used in gathering a herd

of these Longhorns, to form a nucleus with which steers driven out of the brush might consent to remain while most of the cowboys went back to "round up" more cattle. "These cattle," wrote Jim Cook of a decoy herd, "were not what would have been called gentle in any part of the United States, save southern Texas. They had been separated from the wild herds, and were 'gentle' to just the extent that they had become accustomed to the sight of a man on horseback."

As the cattle remained hidden in the brush during the daytime, only venturing out on the small prairies at night, most of the work of gathering had to be done early in the morning, commencing an hour or two before daylight. About two hours before dawn the cook would shout out "Chuck!" and the boss, up at the word, anxious to see his herd increase, might yell, "Breakfast, boys! Damn you, get up!" two or three times. Breakfast over, the cowboys would saddle the ponies "staked out" the night before, and strike out for a small prairie perhaps three or four miles from camp, leaving two or three cowboys behind to bring with them the herd already gathered.

Once at the edge of the "flat," the cowboys would dismount and wait for the grazing cattle to begin to move toward the timber that was their hiding-place. With the first appearance of daylight the cattle would turn their heads toward the nearest bit of timber, and begin grazing at a lively rate. Then the cowboys, remounted, circled through the brush to reach that point. Once there they uncoiled their ropes and rode out to meet the herd. A vigilant old-timer among the Longhorns would perhaps spy the riders before they had ridden twenty feet from the timber; then the whole herd would follow him in his angry rush forward. Each cowboy would "spot" one of the finest cows in the bunch (all cattle were "cows," in range parlance), and attempt to dodge the other cows while he roped and tied down that particular one. When the previously gathered herd arrived, it would be driven to each one of the tied-down cows. Once the cowboy had untied the ropes and warily retreated, the cow would run into the herd, usually to stay there contented.

On moonlit nights the same strategy might be worked just after the cattle had left the brush and were grazing on the prairie. Once the boss had given the signal, every rider was off at top speed "for anything in the shape of a cow brute he could locate."

One end of the rope was tied to the saddle-horn, a requirement of the Texas tradition. "When a rider had his noose around a big animal's horns, neck, or body, and the animal rushed around one side of a tree while rider and horse went on the opposite side, something had to happen," wrote a cowboy. "Either the rope snapped or there was a collision about half the rope-length from the tree."

The anticipation of an Indian raid with each full moon, and the danger of attack regardless of the moon that attended a party of cowboys on camp, made the Texans light-sleeping, quick-fingered, always wary; it made them the best of cowboys, ready for any test of endurance or of skill that the cow-country had to offer.

At the close of the Civil War every ranch or village in the northwestern third of Texas was subject to an Indian raid every full moon; the Indians were always anxious to secure guns, pistols, knives, and were willing to ambush a few white men or Mexicans with or without hope of plunder. Cowboys in camp would sleep some distance apart and away from the campfire, as Indians might slip up to send a shower of lead or arrows. "A snoring man was an abomination in the cow camp," Captain

Cook remembered. "If we cared for the life of such a man, we almost felt we had to guard him while he slept."

Under such conditions, "fighting his way with knife and gun," the Texas cowboy was evolved, a fearless rider, a workman of sublime self-confidence, unequalled in the technique and the tricks of "cowpunching," the most accurate on the trigger and the last to leave untasted the glass which the bartender silently refilled. When the northern trails became an institution the Texan was trail-boss and straw-boss; and as boss he was dictator. As an underling he was not so successful in the north; with a Yankee boss, or worse yet an Englishman, he cherished a studied disregard for authority, and an assured satisfaction in the superiority of his own ways. His loyalty to his profession made him willing to do any amount of work in the line of duty; but he would have defended with his gun his right to sing as he rode:

Oh, I am a Texan cowboy,
Far away from home,
If ever I get back to Texas
I never more will roam.

CHAPTER TWO

COWBOY AND COOK

AT a little railway-station of the cattle-country a young man in striking regalia might swing down from the car steps, breathe deep of God's free air, offer a tribute in one appreciative gaze at the cloudless Western sky, then make inquiry of some depot-lounger of the way to the nearest ranch. The range came to expect and recognize the "mail-order cowboy," who arrived already fitted in cowboy-wear as he knew it from his reading and the assurances of some Middle Western store-keeper—round soft hat, blue silk shirt, leather knee-leggings over laced boots, short straight spurs, and a glistening pistol in a "closed" scabbard. Hardly any one except Englishmen attempted the introduction of knickers.

Cowboy clothing was certainly distinctive, but it had its own rigid conventions. The tenderfoot seldom got as far as "the nearest ranch" before he learned of these; at the railway-town there was a storekeeper ready with kind advice and the right sort of outfit, to be sold to the tenderfoot at a comfortable profit.

"If you wish to put on style, and at the same time have a serviceable outfit, you can invest $500 very handy," advised Charlie Siringo in 1886; but such costly outfits were to be purchased only in western Texas or in Mexico. A saddle with silver inlaid and filigreed might cost three hundred dollars, but one "flashy" yet serviceable could be bought for a hundred, with another hundred for a silver-mounted bridle and spurs to match. Fifty dollars for a gold-mounted sombrero, the high-crowned hat of the Mexicans, another fifty for a saddle blanket, and twenty-five for a quirt and a lariat (*la reata,* "the rope," from the Spanish) helped to make the five hundred vanish. A Colt "45" would cost fifty dollars if it were pearl-handled and gold-mounted, an ornate Winchester rifle would take seventy-five more, and a pair of chaps ("skeleton overalls," Rollins has called them) of thick goat's wool, would leave twenty-five dollars. This would buy a cow-pony.

Such luxurious adornment was not for the tenderfoot, of course. His humble social position in the range-world and his purse alike

SPANISH VAQUERO—THE FIRST AMERICAN COWBOY

urged him to cheaper stuff. In a large cow-town a pony and saddle could each be had for twenty-five dollars, and leather chaps, a hat, and saddle-blankets, all for fifteen dollars. A serviceable Colt '45" could be bought for twelve dollars.

Especially if the cowboy expected to make a trip up the trail, he added a raincoat. "What a blessing to cowmen was the old yellow slicker!" exclaimed a reminiscent old-timer. By possessing a horse, saddle and bridle of his own, the cowboy gained an independence of his ranch which he found pleasant; but with blankets and quirt he was not always as particular.

The cowboy did not often wear a coat, but he always wore a vest. Its main justification was the storage room it provided. More cowboys smoked cigarettes than smoked pipes; and the little round "Bull" sign dangling from a vest-pocket was almost a medal for the fraternity of Westerners. For the eyes of his lady-love and for dances and celebrations the well-dressed cowboy had an extra vest, a sartorial masterpiece, plush or rough wool, dyed in the grand fashion, solid color and plenty of it. Some decorative pattern might entwine itself against this background, and a straight or scalloped braid most likely edged the creation.

Most cowboys wore Stetsons, gray, black, or brown—hats whose crowns were sometimes eight inches in height, whose brims at noonday gave shade beyond the cowboys' shoulders. Sometimes the brim was tipped with silken braid; sometimes along its outer edge the cowboy cut a row of slits through which he twined a strip of leather or a piece of wire, either for ornament or to keep the brim from sagging. This wide brim shaded the cowboy's eyes from the sun as he worked, and again when he found time to lie on the grass at midday for an hour of sleep. "In rainy weather," writes Philip Rollins, "it served as an umbrella. The brim, when grasped between the thumb and fingers and bent into a trough, was on its upper surface the only drinking-cup of the outdoors; when pulled down and tied over the ears, it gave complete protection from frost-bite. It fanned into activity every camp fire started in the open, and enlarged the carrying capacity of the hat when used as a pail to transport water for extinguishing embers." About the crown ran a band—a leather band, as it usually came from the factory at Philadelphia to the cow-town storekeeper; but the cowboys—

Texans especially—often had this belt replaced with one of gold or silver wires, or had the leather studded with round silver plates, *conchas;* and in the Southwest sometimes the store-band was thrown away and the skin of a rattlesnake twisted about the base of the crown. The crown itself was indented by the wearer's thumbs as his own fancy, guarded by the custom of his own range, suggested; in general the crown was worn at its full height in the Southwest and crushed on the top in the Northern ranges.

A red bandanna folded diagonally hung loosely about its wearer's neck. "Tail riders," cowboys who rode in the rear of moving cattle-herds to keep the stragglers in the procession, protected themselves from the dust by pulling their bandannas up to their eyes. Against snow and sleet and wind the bandanna offered like protection; and the cowboy wore it always.

Gloves of fine buckskin (sometimes of leather or horse-hide) were worn all the year—throughout the winter, for warmth, and in summer as a protection against the burn of a hurtling lariat. Some cowboys—"top hands," usually—always wore gloves, a subtle advertisement that the wearer, skilled in riding and in roping, was never called upon for coarse manual labor. The gloves usually had wrist-gauntlets with a flare of about five inches, fringed with metal wires or silken thread. On the gauntlet the Lone Star or some other design was often stenciled or woven.

Chaps, worn when there was riding to be done, were also a part of the cowboy's courtin'-clothes. Those same cowboys that always wore gloves might keep their chaps on always, as a trick of vanity. Englishmen, and a few ranch-owners who were making too much money, sometimes appeared in knickers. Philip Rollins has suggested the cowboy's barbed aversion to these short pants by quoting one Kansas Evans: "Bill, what 'je think? Yesterday, up to that English outfit's ranch, I seen a grown man walkin' around in boy's knee pants. And they say he's second cousin to a dook. Gosh! Wonder what the dook wears."

A Texas cowboy might wear a silk sash about his waist, in the style of the Spanish ranchero, throughout his days on the range. When Charlie Siringo retired to become a store-keeper in Caldwell, Kansas, he still wore his cowboy boots and his red silk sash. "Finally my silk sash disappeared, and another couldn't be purchased in this northern country. There was nothing to do but wear suspenders to keep my pants up, which almost broke my heart."

There was pleasant opportunity for elaboration in the details of dress, as vanity suggested. Gold and silver trimmings might be added to saddle, bridle, blankets, boots, sombrero. Spurs might have "jingle-bobs" to tinkle as the cowboy walked; and Mexican spurs with rowels of two inches or more in length, worn in Texas as a matter of good form, when worn in the Northwest advertised as effectively—and as delusively—as hotel-stickers on a valise the experience of the owner. The cowboy's boots were a traditional expression of ethnic pride—of fine leather, with thin, narrow soles, high heels, binding the feet in an effeminately uncomfortable fit. "He is proud that he is a horseman, and he has contempt for all human beings who walk. . . . The cowboy does not walk, and he is proud of the fact," explains Hough. "On foot in his tight, stumpy, tight-toed boots he is lost. But he wishes you to understand that he is never on foot." Cowboys took great pride in their small feet, and though when on the trail with a restless herd the boots might have to be worn night and day for perhaps a fortnight, no amount of discomfort was held to justify surrendering the illusion.

When the cowboy slept in the ranch-house

he took off just as much of his clothing as he cared, the degree of exposure regulated not by convention but by temperature. No cowboy wore nightgown or pajamas, of course. On the trail, some day when the cattle had been bedded near a stream in early evening, all the cowboys but a few who rode guard on the herd would go to the river's edge, strip, and wash their clothes and themselves as well. If there were extra topshirts and undershirts in the blanket-rolls or in a corner of the cook's wagon, well and good. If there were not, a brush fire could quickly dry both cowboys and clothes.

The gun was the ultimate item in cowboy adornment. Indispensable in the days when Indian raids were always to be feared, even after those days it was convenient to own one (a range aphorism had to do with the gun of the Texan: He didn't need it often, but when he did, he needed it like hell), and tradition dictated that it be carried as an item of formal dress even when its two and a quarter pounds was a useless burden. When Jim Cook came into Texas, early in the history of the trail, "Everybody went armed to the teeth at all hours. No man removed more than his coat or brush jacket when he lay down to sleep. There was danger on all sides, and from many sources." To be "armed to the teeth" meant to carry a brace of revolvers and to have a Winchester rifle strapped to one's saddle. An occasional bad man in later days when "two-gun men" were familiar nuisances in some of the cow-towns might carry a third gun, strapped under one shoulder; but such walking arsenals were freaks, and usually cowards as well.

The Colt pistol was referred to as a gun, sometimes as a "cutter"; while on a "quiet" range this gun was generally carried in the blanket-roll, the cowboy wore it on holiday trips to town or to a neighboring ranch, and on other occasions when he was on his dignity. Familiar with his gun from using it on "objectionable animals from snakes upwards," the cowboy had a natural propensity to toy with it in moments of careless ease or whisky-incited exuberance. Writes Stewart Edward White, "I stopped for supper at the Circle I ranch. While waiting for dinner I lay on my back in the bunk-room and counted three hundred and sixty-two bullet holes in the ceiling. They came to be there because the festive cowboys used to while away the time lying as I was lying while waiting for supper, in shooting the flies that crawled about the plaster."

When the cowboy had mastered his business, he could command *good* wages—twenty-five to sixty dollars a month, the amount contingent largely on the latitude, with wages progressively higher as the Canadian border was approached. Cowpunching was not, certainly, a lucrative profession; and the trail-drivers saved least of all. Bringing the cattle north to the annual market, working for perhaps thirty dollars a month and railroad fare back, meant a glorious opportunity to spend whatever of the trip's wages that was not owed before it was received, in the pleasures offered by the cow-towns at the end of the drive. An old cowboy epitomized his trail-driving days thus: "The next spring I would have the same old trip, the same old things would happen in the same old way, and with the same old wind-up. I put in eighteen or twenty years on the trail, and all I had in the outcome was the high-heeled boots, the striped pants and about $4.80 worth of other clothes, so there you are."

The cook presided over his stove in the rear of the one big room that was the typical ranch-house in the north; in the Southwest the kitchen was usually a room to itself, connecting with the ranch-house. On the trail-drives the cook, with his chuck-wagon, was an essential adjunct.

The chuck-wagon was a royal chamber on wheels; the cook was the autocrat of the trail, by virtue of the sublime necessity of his office. The one delicacy of his *cuisine* was pie, always of dried or canned apples enclosed in the sort of crust that only a range cook dared to make. Beans and bacon, with canned tomatoes or some other canned vegetable by way of variety, and Spanish onions as a relish, were his staples. A stray yearling furnished fresh meat; the cowboy "sopped" his "chunk" of beef and his bread in a pan of gravy. Coffee, usually without sugar and always without cream, was the universal drink. In pretentious ranches in the northern country canned milk was sometimes used on the cattleman's table.

"Too much praise or credit cannot be given to those old-time trail cooks who were numbered among the good ones," writes a cowboy. There were some like the old negro who cooked for Siringo's outfit in 1871, whose meals were generally of meat from a fat heifer—often two kinds at once, ribs broiled before the camp fire, and an ovenful of loin, sweetbreads, and heart, mixed in gravy—with cornbread, molasses, and black coffee; and for breakfast pork and beans which had been simmering over hot coals all night. Only a very few attained the

TRAIL COOK

badness of that young man whom James Gibson remembers, who turned cook when he found no other opening. Given dried apples to cook for pie, he filled the pot full and covered them with water; to his consternation this strange fruit began to swell and overflow the pot. A cowboy passing saw him frantically digging a hole in the sand, and burying the surplus apples as they pushed over. "At first the coffee was all grounds, the bread like leather, and the beans rattled down one's throat, but being a persevering kind of a fellow, by the next roundup he had become a really good cook."

The immediate *entourage* of the wagons was under the absolute control of the cook. Cowboys who staked out their horses too close to his domain, or night-riders who disturbed his peace of mind by riding among the sleeping cowboys to find and wake the next on guard, were marked for discipline. Practiced in mild grumbling, when he chose to become vicious in his wit his ridicule paralyzed the defense of most cowboys. And there were other, more subtle ways of punishment. The coffee might suddenly become lamentably insipid, the cooking even worse than was usual. By such tyranny the cook might coerce the whole outfit into becoming his allies and subduing the offender. Whenever the cook could show that a cowboy had by some carelessness jarred the decorum of the kitchen and cast discredit on his profession, the rest of the outfit might avenge the dignity of their calling by a "chapping"—a laying on of leather after the manner of ancient disciplinarians, the offender's own pair of chaps sometimes the instrument.

The cook never took part in the management of the cattle, unless he was allowed to "swop places" with one of the cowboys, as a rare diversion. He was seldom a good rider, and in one cowboy's words, the sight of the "old lady" on a cow-pony loping up and down beside the cattle, "is a striking contrast to the dignity he exhibits in the kneading of an ash cake or the broiling of a slice of 'sow belly.' "

Inevitably associated with the cowboy is the cowboy's horse; in the life on the range as well as in the sentimental ballads, there has been a bond between horse and man based on the necessities of range work, and on something more subtle than the bare requirements of labor. Part of the story of the West is the story of horses and horse-wranglers.

CHAPTER THREE

THE COWBOY'S MOUNT

A STOUT-BELLIED veteran of the cattle-country was once asked to define a cowboy. He answered, after the pause prescribed by the best range custom, "A cowboy is a man with guts and a horse." The cattle-country guffawed appreciatively, and has been repeating the joke ever since; but there are some "cowboys" now in the West guiding tractors through alfalfa fields, who do not laugh at it any more.

Wild horses of the plains, descendants of the Spanish horses that had escaped from the *conquistadores* of the sixteenth century, had spread from Mexico into Texas, and on into the great plains bordering the Rockies.

The Spanish mustang caught in Texas in the early days of the cattle trade might be a thoroughbred. A spirited pony that outran and outwitted his pursuers earned the admiration of the cowboys on the frontier; but his fine independence challenged the superiority of man, and he was a marked animal. Some of these wild horses gained a reputation over the

MEXICAN SADDLE

entire Texas range; and when Berry Robuck boasted in his retirement, "I am the man who caught the blue mustang mare," he did not have to retell the story to his fellow-cowboys at the Trail Drivers' convention. With the coming of the cowboys the White Steed of the Prairies came into the national folk-lore, a superb, free stallion, the quintessence of fine horseflesh, the idealization of cowboys who cared more for their mounts than they would have told.

Until the early eighties, the cowboy's horses were most likely bred in Texas. Remarkably tough but generally small, they were called cow-ponies. Under a cowboy's saddle, which weighed from thirty-five to forty pounds, with perhaps a "beefy" cowboy astride him, the cow-pony seemed lost under his burden; but the cowboy knew that a compactly built pony about fourteen hands high worked better and longer than might a larger animal. Nor did temper vary according to weight. One horse as docile as any movie cowboy could wish might be of the same size and build as another who bucked with or without provocation.

The cowboy usually preferred one that would buck occasionally—a pleasant but usually ineffectual exhibition of spirit that in the end emphasized the cowboy's supremacy.

With the opening of the northern ranges, the Texas cowboys that had come "up the trail" to the northern markets no longer had to drive their ponies back into Texas; and for a few years, until the upper ranges had a comfortable supply of their own, Texas was something of a breeding ground for the entire range. It was here that the profession of horse-breaking really developed, with the year's supply of horses taken up the trail for the constant use of the cowboys and sold when a buyer was found in the cow-town terminus. At the price of ponies in Texas, this was a profitable side-line:

Oh, a ten-dollar hoss and a forty-dollar saddle,
And I'm goin' to punchin' Texas cattle.

But the cow-ponies did not always cost as much as ten dollars, though eighteen was a frequent price for the pick of a bunch. "Shanghai" Pierce once brought three hundred Mexican ponies, "wet ponies," into Texas, at a cost of two dollars and fifty cents a head. "Shanghai" was one of many cattlemen that traded occasionally in "wet ponies." A deal would be entered into for a number of geldings to be put in the river on the Mexican side. Accordingly ponies stolen by organized Mexican thieves from the herds in Old Mexico would be forced into the Rio Grande; and all those that swam over to the Texas side would be paid for by the purchaser.

With the cowboys of each ranch usually breaking in the horses for the home ranch, certain cowboys demonstrated a particular gift for this kind of work that made them known in the near-by ranches. These men gradually became a class by themselves, "bronco busters," who followed the trade of horse-breaking, at so much a horse, or who stayed on the home ranch at an advanced salary. A cattleman caught in this transition period when differentiation in the work of the range was beginning who did not grant the demand for extra pay might find himself without the services of his top hands. "You see, he expected us to ride a horse a few times until he began to get docile and then turn him over to one of his muley pets while we caught up a fresh one," was a valid excuse on the range for "riding out" on a boss.

As the cattle-country of the West became less dependent on Texas, restive cowboys of these ranges set out "on their own" to capture the wild horses of the plains—not the typical mustang stock that cowboys rode up the trail from Texas, for these had mingled with horses abandoned by plainsmen. If the mares were to be captured, the stallion that led them must be captured or killed. A cowboy on horseback could not hope to overtake and rope the wild stallions; and if the cowboy could not get within range to shoot, or was one of that fine sentimental sort that would not lift his gun to kill these horses, a whole winter's campaign, in which elaborate traps were used, might be necessary.

Then, whether the captors were independent "horse men" or were cowboys assigned to catch the wild horses because they were harmful to the peace of mind of the range stock, there came the work of "horse-busting."

The work involved in breaking a horse depended on the temperament of the animal and the requirement of the service for which the horse was designed. A horse for the use of that phantom of delight, the owner's niece out for a summer's visit, suffered a long period of careful treatment, which might or might not transform the native strain of wildness; but the horse-buster who got four or five dollars a head did little more than prove ocularly that a particular horse "could actually be mounted and ridden without death to either horse or man." Roosevelt, reviewing his experiences in the Little Missouri country, wrote "In the cow-country there is nothing more refreshing than the light-hearted belief entertained by the average man to the effect that any animal which by main force has been saddled and ridden, or harnessed and driven a couple of times, is a 'broke horse.' My present foreman is firmly wedded to this idea, as well as to its complement, the belief that any animal with hoofs, before any vehicle with wheels, can be driven across any country."

The simple object of bucking was to get rid of the rider. A horse usually started by putting his head between his legs, arching his back after the manner of an angry cat, raising all four legs for one exhilarating jump, and descending with a nerve-rending jar. If he were a sincere but unimaginative bucker, he might continue in just this fashion until he was quite worn out; the most intelligent buckers could display an almost unlimited repertoire of variety and invention. Sudden lunges of a shoulder or hip, miraculous convulsions of the spine, jumps rearward or sideways, all had a tendency to sort riders into the class who stayed on, and the class who didn't. Siringo describes his experience with a "wet pony," a large iron-gray, whom the Mexicans pointed out as "Mucho Diablo." "None of the boys cared to tackle him. So one morning I caught and saddled him. He fought like a tiger while being saddled, and after getting it securely fastened he threw it off and stamped it into a hundred pieces, with his front feet, which caused me to have to buy a new one next day. I then borrowed Mr. Stephen's saddle, and after getting securely seated in it, raised the blinds and gave him the full benefit of spurs and quirt. After pitching about half a mile, me, saddle and all went up into the air, the girths having broken. But having the 'hackimore' rope fastened to my belt I held to him until help arrived. I then borrowed another saddle, and this time I stayed with him."

Siringo's "hackimore" (his spelling is his own) was a bridle which had no bit, but a rawhide or horsehair ring that could be slipped around the horse's head just above his mouth. Adjusted loosely, the hackamore gave the rider a minimum of control; that was why the cowboy liked it.

The cowboy quoted as having said, "Bucking started from the back door of hell on a hot day, and came out on the run," did not care to remember, lest he spoil his little joke, that the horse with spirit enough to buck occasionally was also the horse with "cow sense," that understood the ways of cows and anticipated the directions of his driver with a liveliness not due to any human guidance.

"A horse is not trained to buck, as some folks think; out there on the open range he already knows how," writes a cowboy. This knowledge, range logic concluded, was a heritage of the old conflicts between horse and wolf, and horse and mountain lion, before men came to tame the horse and shoot down the wolf and the lion. Legend harkened to a peerless stallion, "Comet," who escaped with his little coterie of mares from the Spaniards, and started a wild bunch of high-blooded mustangs that grazed over half a continent. "And when the cowpuncher's loop spreads over the mustang's head and draws up, he's fighting the same as he would with the cougar, he's a bucking, striking, kicking, and biting hunk of horseflesh to anything that's close."

The "jug-head" seemed never to remember his hazing of the day before. "He's got to be pulled around a heap, and it takes a lot of elbow grease to get him lined out for anything," noted James. Of the worst horse on the range, the "killer," the cowboy-historian says, "He's the kind of horse with a far-away look. Some folks call 'em locoed. But whether he's that or not he'll sure take a man through some awful places and sometimes only one comes out. That horse is out to get his man and he don't care if he gets himself while doing

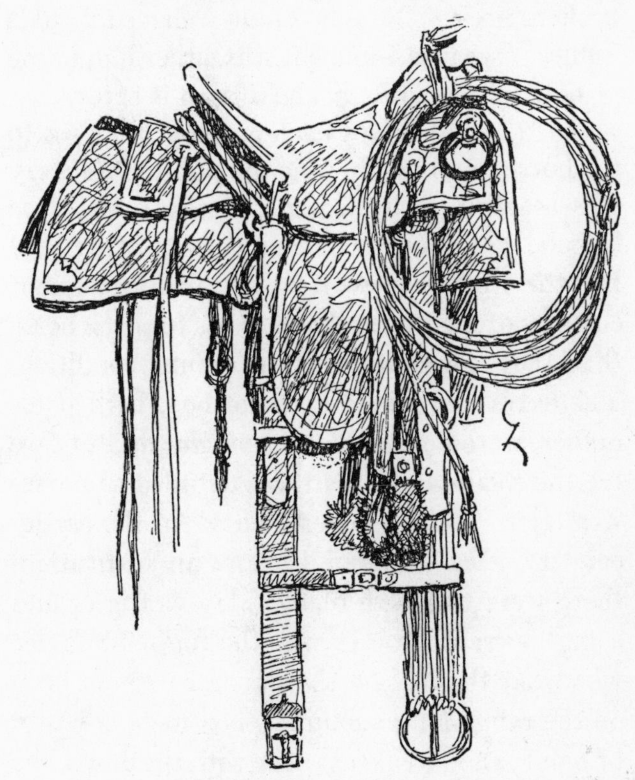

PRESENT-DAY TEXAS SADDLE

the getting." James pulled the saddle off such a horse once after a hard ride, when the horse suddenly whirled, kicking, snapping, biting at the hackamore, ran past the cowboy, and headed straight for the side of the corral; he butted the bars squarely, and fell back with a broken neck. "I felt kinda relieved," adds James, "because I knew it was either him or me or both of us had to go; he'd tried it before."

On the trail-drives each cowboy used six to ten horses, and by the time the point of delivery was reached perhaps none of them would be in good condition. With no corn or other feed but the wild grasses, it was only by frequent changes of mounts and long rests for each horse that they could be kept in riding condition. The extra mounts of each cowboy, herded together, were known as the *remuda;* and to care for the *remuda* one man was detailed as horse-wrangler. With the "efficiency" of the cattle-country once the trail became an institution, there were two such men, a day-wrangler and a night-wrangler. It was the night-wrangler who woke the cook, if that laborer had not been on the range long enough to become a creature of habit; and, breakfast over with the dawn, the wrangler would drive the *remuda* near the camp, and hold the rope, with a cowboy at the other end, that formed an improvised corral, while the cowboys threw their lariats over those horses they had selected for beginning the day's work. Then the remnant was led away by the wrangler, perhaps to be driven up again at the noon camp for those that needed new mounts. In the days of a single wrangler the cowboy "staked out" each night the horse he intended for the next morning's work, and held the *remuda* overnight in a rope corral. Range custom varied in the details of horse-wrangling, and in the status of the wrangler; in one camp he might be lower than the fledglings who "rode tail" on the herd, and in another second in authority to the foreman.

A delectable generalisation much in vogue conceives of the typical cowboy as a lover of horses, one who fed his favorite mount sugar whenever he might steal it from the cook, one ready to drub with his fists the vicious exception who maltreated his horses. But the horse was simply a part of the great machinery of the cattle-country; and how the cowboy chose to use his horses was purely his own business provided that the work on hand was done. Charlie Siringo, in 1886, might remember that the six horses he rode up the trail in 1877 were named Comanche, Allisan, Last Chance, Creeping Moses, Damfido, and Beat-and-be-Damned; but Charlie Siringo had worked side by side with many a cowboy who selected a horse from his string almost at random, slapped his saddle on a back that might be a mass of open sores, and quirted and spurred his horse as he rode all day—if not in deliberate cruelty, in complete indifference.

The foreman of an outfit, knowing from experience the value of a *remuda* in good condition, and most likely from Texas where the cowboys named their horses (a custom almost lost on the northern ranges in the eighties), was ready to discharge the cowboy he found to be a "horse mauler" when he could easily be replaced; if a horse mauler were retained, he would most likely be given a string picked by the foreman, of the most intractable horses in the *remuda.* These horses were in every bunch, but like the horse maulers were in a minority among their kind; they were qualified to fight back, and if for part of the drive the cook's wagon carried a cowboy with a broken leg, that cowboy was usually the one in the outfit least considerate of his horses.

Even the hackamore, least troublesome to the horse of all controlling devices, might be placed so that each pull would bring smothering pressure on the horse's nostrils, and bring great agony if the horse continued to strain on the rope. At the other extreme was the vicious Spanish spade-bit, pressing on the tongue when it rested, and forcing metal against the soft parts of the horse's mouth when the bridle was jerked. No western-story writer has cared to describe horse-breaking as it was often practiced when the northern outfits were systematized, with the professional bronco buster beating the horse with a quirt about the head and shoulders, while two cowboys assisted by quirting its flanks, before the horse-breaker mounted, to glorify his performance then by raking his spurs in bloody tracks from the horse's shoulders to its hips.

In later days maltreating horses has often been profitable; for the more vicious the horse the greater the price he brings from the managers of rodeos and frontier-day celebrations. The number of atavistic horses that buck, strike, and bite is becoming less and less, and must be supplemented by horses deliberately "spoiled."

Admiration of a rider for his horse might develop into affection, especially if the cowboy were allowed to keep the same string of horses for the length of his stay with one outfit; but since range work required treble the number of men in summer that it needed in winter, the foreman had often to redistribute the mounts in the *remuda,* and a cow-pony might have a new master for each year.

The one or two particularly lively and clever horses in his string might be kept by the cowboy for special occasions, as in roundup work, when he had opportunity to "show off." The cowboy on a pony that would approach a herd without guidance from the reins and divine from the slightest pressure of the rider's knee what cow was to be cut out, working that cow to the edge of the herd, using only his own "cow sense" for direction, and perhaps snap at the cow's shanks to hurry it on, deserved and received admiration. Wrote a cowboy rich in experience, "As for brains and honesty—I hate to compare a dog or any other animal with the deep-hearted, long-winded pony of the Western ranges."

Horse-stealing was never as general or as successful as cattle-rustling; the interests of the cowboy were too directly affected by the loss of his horse for any amount of sentimentality to mitigate the offense. In the late eighties the more daring of the lawless element that drifted into Wyoming, choosing between two careers, decided that whereas rustling cattle meant brand-altering and slow moving, horses could be moved swiftly and in large bands to some hiding-place where they might wait comfort-

CALIFORNIA-NEVADA STYLE SADDLE

ably for a purchaser. "How many horses travelled over this Outlaw Trail has never been known; but old-timers in the Wind River country tell of seeing two hundred go past in a single band," records Frederick Bechdolt. In Wyoming, by 1890, the horse-rustlers who harassed the big stockmen had the secret support of the small cattlemen, and it was almost impossible to get a jury to convict. Nevada became a rendezvous for horse-thieves and cattle-rustlers; and a strange rider, "spotted" as most likely a sheriff, might ride up to a ranch and find it deserted, the cowboys having left their work to ride down some gully for safety.

Such conditions could not last long anywhere; and when the courts failed, vigilantes provided the answer.

There is a story of a certain vigilante in the Southwest who had supervised the hanging of several undesirable citizens, horse-thieves prominent among them. Summoned to appear as special venireman for a murder trial, he had to answer to the district attorney's statutory question, "Have you any conscientious scruples in regard to the infliction of the punishment of death for crime?" And the "Captain" answered, "I have." From the silence that followed he felt that some explanation was due: "Judge, it's this a-way. I don't want to hang a man unless I've got something agin him."

That horse-stealing was the most heinous crime in the code of the West is flamboyant nonsense that seemingly will not die; but the malice of one who would steal a cowboy's horse was too contemptible for the cow-country to endure.

CALIFORNIA SPUR

CHAPTER FOUR

THE ROUNDUP

"IT'S lay close to old Con's flank, kid, and keep your end up or turn in your string of horses. On the roundup no soldiering goes; sick or well, it's hit yourself in the flank with your hat and keep up with the bunch or be set afoot to pack up your saddle; there's no room in the chuck wagon for a quitter's blankets, and no time to close herd sick ones. So for heaven's sake, don't start out unless you have the guts to stand it."

And the novice, perhaps a farmer's son lured west by garish reports of the ease of the cowboy's work and the wickedness of his pleasures, found himself at once thrust into a régime of long hours, hard work, and little sleep. Perhaps weekly excursions on a broad-flanked mare to town for supplies and mail had been the extent of his riding before he invested his patrimony in horse, gun, and trimmings; but there was no easy apprenticeship in becoming a cowboy. The roundup was boom time in the cattle-country, and it demanded treble the number of men that held range employment through the winter. A reunion for the old cowboys, this twin-spectacle of the Trail was also the initiation of most tenderfeet.

The roundup had come out of the East. A thin population in the mountain-country of the lower Alleghanies had long permitted its cattle to run at large; and at the full of each spring the owners held a roundup, a gathering-in, of their scattered herds, with such of the year's crop of calves as had escaped the wolves and other prowling beasts of the country.

The calves were branded, such cows as were wanted were driven away, and the remainder was again turned loose upon the hills. The emigrants from the Cumberland country into Texas brought knowledge of this institution with them; but until after the Civil War there was little call to improve on the desultory system of the Mexican *vaquero,* who rode out on the range with a branding-iron strapped to his saddle, and once among the cattle branded such as he could catch, until he became tired and rode back to the ranch.

But when cattle became more valuable and ranchmen became more numerous, each ranchman came to have a personal interest in his neighbor's roundup; some of his own cattle had wandered far in their winter's roamings, and if the calves were to bear their rightful brand it were best to send one or two of his own cowboys to attend this neighbor's roundup. A cowboy was loyal to his employer, and not always careful in his zeal that each calf he branded followed a cow bearing the brand of his boss. The outcome was that squads of five, ten, or more cowboys, representing a group of neighboring cattlemen, skirmished the range-country about a ranch, while another squad representing the same owners used another ranch, with its corral, or enclosure, as a base for gathering in the cattle. The cowboys in each squad helped each other on the range and in the branding pen; and when they found in their herds "slick ears," as they called those yearlings that had been missed in the round-ups of the season before, they knew about what percentage each was entitled to, and apportioned them out, seldom with any dissatisfaction.

Out of this careful regard for each other's rights came an even more remarkable coöperation; when calves that had followed their mothers far from their native ranges were found, these cowboys would most likely take a "running iron," a straight rod, and trace out the mother's brand on the calves. Of course, when the cook needed beef, these stray calves and their mothers were often parted. This killing of another's steer or heifer when beef was wanted was a stock trick of the range, generally winked at, and excused by the comfortable conviction that matters worked out pretty evenly. One cowboy was fond of relating how his outfit was regaling itself with the choicest portions of a two-year-old heifer, from whose pelt the brand of D3 had just been cut and judiciously concealed, when "old beef-baron D3" himself chanced to ride up, and dismounted for dinner with the outfit. At a pause in the gourmandizing he commented on the quality of the beef, almost as good as D3 beef itself—in fact, he added, "it tastes powerful like it." And the foreman retorted, "I'll bet you a horse this is the first time you ever tried that taste."

When Jim Cook was a tenderfoot on the Texas range, he was ordered to kill a cow for beef. A fat heifer wandering by itself appeared to him a fine choice, and he had pointed his carbine when his boss rode toward him, fairly yelling, "Hold on, young man, don't you see that's a T Diamond?"

" 'Yes,' I replied. 'What brand is that?'

" 'I reckon that's my brand,' was the answer. 'We don't kill that kind in this country. Kill an L O W or a W B G'—meaning any one's brand but his own. 'They taste better.' "

The makeshift roundups of these early Texans, which ended with a ranchman's cowboys in each squad driving his cattle back to the home range, were supplanted by a definite system of rounding-up by districts. In 1877 the cattlemen of western Texas arranged for district roundups; and as state-wide associations of cattlemen became the fashion, the roundup was systematized in a high degree.

A roundup boss, some experienced and respected cowman, was chosen at a spring meeting of the stockowners. Each of these cattlemen furnished cowboys and bore a share of the expenses in proportion to the number of cattle he owned, or thought he owned. The date of the roundup, some time in May or June, when the grass had become plentiful and the calves large enough to be branded, was chosen by the roundup boss. On northern ranges where Texans were outnumbered, the roundup boss might successfully insist on being called the superintendent.

Two or three days before the date set, the

outfits would begin to assemble. In a large district over two hundred men might come together by the date of the roundup; and each outfit had its *remuda* (more often, in the northern ranges, called "cavva-yard," from the Spanish *caballado*) of some seven or nine extra mounts for each cowboy, and perhaps a chuck-wagon with its bulky plunder.

As early as three-thirty in the morning the day of work began, with the cook's call for breakfast. Perhaps it was simply "Come an' get it," but there have been cooks with talents not confined to breadmaking and swearing, who varied the formula to suit their virtuosity, as did one Wiley, whose call was, "Come, boys, get up and hear the little birds sing their sweet praises to God Almighty; damn your souls, get up!"

There was no delaying on this matin. The cook's fire blazed near the chuck-wagon; and a very few minutes after the call the cowboys would be gathered about, each of them with a tin plate on which the cook slapped meat and bread, and a tin cup that he filled with coffee "strong enough to float an egg."

Once the second or third cup of black coffee had been gulped down, each cowboy roped and saddled his horse from the *remuda,* which had been driven up to camp as a signal that there was no more time for breakfasting. As the cowboys rode away and over the prairie they spread out, breaking up into small groups, each with its own boss, as the superintendent had directed.

"We cross the river at a wild spot. . . . A steep narrow gorge leads to wide plains, bounded by a low range of flat-topped antelope hills. Up this gorge the circle-riders make their way, and dividing into couples, start at a lope for the lurking-places of the cattle. Creek, shady canyon, and arroyo are searched, and after many a chase after wilful calf or sullen bull, a goodly roundup . . . is formed." In rough country where each little ravine must be searched and each knoll circled, each group of "circle-riders" would be smaller than groups in unbroken plains country. At the lope of the cow-pony this intricate following of cattle-tracks and bypaths held some danger. An Easterner with a lively curiosity saw a spill down a steep hillside, when a horse thrust his foreleg into a gopher-hole and threw his rider a distance the Easterner measured as "thirty-seven feet less three inches." The cowboy was only slightly injured. He picked himself up, "and pulling his six-shooter forthwith, shot the disabled broncho." There the enthusiastic narrator ends; but under ordinary circumstances there must have been a sequel for the cowboy—a walk of several miles back to camp.

By noon or shortly after the day's rounding-up had been finished, and the cattle each group of circle-riders had gathered were thrown into one herd. Around the dusty, milling, bawling herd of golden duns, murky yellows, reds and piebalds, the cowboys rode to drive back the cows that tried to dash out from the edge.

Then came the sorting-out process, the cowboys of each ranch "cutting out" the cattle of one brand, with the calves that followed; and the great aggregation was broken up into a number of small herds a quarter-mile or less apart.

The cowboy enjoyed the cutting-out, if there were not too much of it. Mounted on a "cutting pony" that was a "Joe-dandy," he made a figure for his boss and his fellow cowboys to admire. Some horses seemed never to understand cutting-out after any amount of teaching; but with a "show horse" the rider could hold the reins at the end of his little finger, or perhaps let them lie over the saddle-horn. Once that cow-pony knew, by some almost invisible twitch of the reins or by the pressure of a knee, what cow was wanted, he would urge that animal with deceptive listlessness toward the rim of the herd, when with one sudden spring he could send the cow out at a breakneck gait. If the cow made a perverse attempt to enter the herd that an hour before had been so distasteful, the horse wheeled, always keeping between the cow and the herd, until the contest was settled. Sometimes, of course, the best of cutting ponies failed, if it were tired and overheated, or if the cow became angry and attempted fight.

Before cutting-out began the herd was allowed to remain undisturbed until the cows that had been separated from their calves in the pandemonium of the gathering had time to find their strayed offspring. The institution of the spring roundup was based on the assumption that a calf followed its mother and thus revealed its ownership. The youngsters, bewildered by the hullabaloo of the roundup, did sometimes follow strange cows. In such a case the cow herself usually adjusted the question of title by tossing the "orphan" on her horns and returning to the *mêlée* to search for her rightful child.

The superintendent had sometimes to watch lest the cowboys of a large stockman, in cutting out a group of cows, did not force among the trailing offspring one or two more calves than there were cows. It was practically a universal rule among the cattlemen themselves that all calves in the roundup should be branded and "earmarked" the same as the mothers, even though there was no representative of that brand at the roundup; but the cowboy's rigid conception of loyalty to his boss occasionally defeated this rule, and caused some loss to the small cattlemen. In the absence of legal machinery to safeguard a cattleman's legitimate interests this service fell upon his cowboys; and sometimes disputes of ownership arose at the branding-fire. With nerves frayed and senses confused by the sweat and blood of the branding, all that often prevented gun-play was the immutable rule that the work must go on.

Perhaps the stockman collected his herd as it was cut out, and drove it to his own corral, there to burn on the calves his brand, his mark of ownership; but more often the calves were roped and dragged to a common branding-fire, where there were many branding-irons, and a system of tallying the work.

A collection of irons representing each stockman in the roundup lay about a blazing fire, over which one or two men worked to keep the brands hot. Expert ropers rode up, each dragging a bawling calf, while its mother stood off at a safe distance and watched. A cowboy at the fire seized the calf by its head or by a fold of skin, turned it over with an upward twist, and quickly secured its legs. Then the brand,

MEXICAN BRANDS

not red-hot but still searing the quivering flesh of the calf, was pressed, and the knife added such additional marks as the owner had adopted further to attest his title. This mark might be a notch cut in an ear, or a cut in some roll of skin—an evidence of servitude spared horses, because it was disfiguring.

For a systematic, seasonal operation, the spectacle seemed strangely crude and confused. The bawling and squirming of the calves and the bellowing of the watching cows was matched by the raucous shouts and the fervid swearing of men running about stripped to the

FAMOUS OLD-TIME BRANDS IN NORTHERN WYOMING AND MONTANA

waist and smeared with blood and dust, branding-iron and knife in hand. The calves could hope for no gentle treatment in such a moil. In an excess of temper not a part of his regular character a cowboy hit by a flying hoof might retaliate with a vicious stab from his knife, or sink his spurred heel against the stomach of the offending calf.

A "tally man" had been appointed by the roundup boss to serve as general bookkeeper; at the branding-fire he stood, keeping record of the calves as they were branded. Perhaps he was an old cowman no longer fit for the long rides to gather the cows nor for the maneuvers of cutting-out from herd; in the earlier days of the range to be tally man was a tribute to one's education. The tally man had opportunity to favor a particular outfit by falsifying his scores, but—to quote Emerson Hough—"this contingency is never considered in the rude ethics of the range, where civilized suspicion, known as conservatism, had not yet fully entered."

As the original herd grew smaller and the marks in the tally-book multiplied, occasionally yearlings without a brand were dragged up to the fire. These were the "mavericks," that had escaped the dragnet of the last year's roundup. Without any sign of ownership upon them, they were distributed according to the niceties of range custom to the different owners in proportion to the size of their herds.

Two men were usually necessary to turn a yearling on its back, though when one man attempted the feat he was sure of ridicule if he failed. But if full-grown cattle were to be branded, the failure of three or four men to hold an animal after he had been thrown down was no shame to them. An old bull "on the prod" had his own way; he could snap with one twist of his head a rope or two thrown over his horns and fastened to a post. The easiest way to brand such a lord of the prairie was in a corral; jammed into a chute the bull could move but slowly, and there was time for a man with a red-hot brand in his hand to press the iron and leave a mark.

The corral was a great convenience in branding—a rough, strongly built enclosure of posts and rails that kept the cattle penned, the calves easily to be taken out and branded just outside the gate. In a drizzling rain the corral could be a very disagreeable place, the cattle churning the earth into spattering mud, the work slow and dirty. Always at branding-time the smell of sweating cattle mingled with the smoke from the fire and the odor of sizzling hair and seared flesh in a pervasive stench more offensive than the smell of sheep (but this the cowboy would not admit).

But the spring roundup was a time to which cowboys and owners looked forward eagerly.

It was a time of renewal of old acquaintance and of cultivating new friendships, of exchanging ballads and hearing tales new and familiar. And in retrospect, at least, work in such a spectacle, however hard it had been, had a satisfying glamor. One ranch boss had found in the spring that not one cow was missing from his range, but he was a young man, not to be done out of his amusement by such an accident. He engaged an unrecommended party to look after his herd in the Medicine Lodge country, and left to attend the roundups going on in the Indian Territory. He found no cattle, of course; but back to his own herd he discovered that under the carelessness of his substitute about half his herd was missing.

There was little time for social amenities in the working-days of the roundup. Then the cowboy needed all the sleep he could get, and soon after supper he selected a place on the ground, went to sleep at will, and probably snored, by a cowboy's description, in "a compound of fog horn and death rattle."

Before the cowboy stretched out his blanket, he pounded hard upon the earth to scare out any lurking rattlesnake or other pest common to that range. Despite such preliminary precautions, however, and despite the Indian-fashion in which the cowboy rolled his blankets about him, he might find in the morning that a nocturnal wanderer or two—snake, scorpion, tarantula, lizard, Gila monster, whatever the climate might supply—had come between him and his blanket for a comfortable night. The danger in entertaining such lodgers was not great, since the cowboy was called to breakfast long before the sun had come to warm the pests into activity.

But because the roundup itself was a stern routine, owners and cowboys were careful to arrive at the spot appointed two or three days before the superintendent had decided rounding-up was to begin. Then, in the dust and confusion of arrival, with horses to be herded, camp to be set, and the blankets and "truck" to be taken out before the cook cleared the wagon with such violence as his temper dictated, yells from camp to camp demanded the Texas Jacks, Frencheys, Kentucks, Hard-boiled Jims, and the Pecos Kids to step forth and be recognized.

As the cowboys rediscovered old acquaintances and shook hands with new ones in the trite ritual they had inherited from the States, they formed small groups for intimate cattle-clatter, of how Bill Johnson's cutting horse pitched his rider into the branding-fire, how Missouri Pete had got peeved at his foreman and turned rustler, how cattle were going to sell that fall, how the dude owner of the Two-Bar M had sold out and gone back East—while tenderfeet on the edge of the group attempted an occasional comment, and the five-cent sacks of tobacco traveled from party to party, a ceremonial of friendship, in unconscious mimicry of one race that on these same plains had gathered for heap-much-talk and had passed the tobacco about. With a lull in the talking poker inevitably was suggested. The urge to poker might travel the length of the camp; then blankets were spread on the ground and progressive poker held the camp for the next few hours. Some who started were "busted;" and others became "busted" as the minutes passed. These played on their honor, the symbol white beans borrowed from the cook.

From the cowboy with a debt of honor aggregating a hatful of beans, to the stockowner with a herd of twenty thousand cattle, the code was the same: each cattleman and each cowboy under him was a man of honor, obligated to a course of equity in range business and fairness in human relations. The many opportunities in these roundups for cheating are easily seen; it is also easily seen, historically, that there are few businesses in which men have been more ready to assist one another than in the old cattle business of the range.

It is significant that as the values of cattle increased the more likely was the owner of thousands of cattle to protect the owner of a few hundreds. The old roundups in Texas had several sharp practices discarded once the cattle business attained magnitude. The men who conducted the early "branding crowds" used a forked pencil, so that for every cow they branded on commission for a neighbor, they received commission for two cows. "But then it turned out all right," an old Texas cowboy has remembered, "as in after years the Eastern speculator, or 'short horn,' began to embark into the stock business with his eyes shut. That is, buying whole 'brands' of cattle out according to the old books. For instance, if the aforesaid widow, or stove-up 'reb,' could show, and prove, that she or he had so many calves branded the *past* season, the buyer would pay for four times as many—that is, counting five head of cattle for every calf branded the year previous. Thus it will be seen that the forked pencil racket proved a blessing to the poor."

CHAPTER FIVE

THE LONG DRIVE NORTH

THE history of the cattle-trail yet to be written will be a story of severe vicissitudes financially, and of a gradual retreat west as homesteaders appropriated its domain and northern cattlemen built enclosures and invoked injunctions to keep back the Texas drives that meant cheaper prices and possibly carried infection to their own cattle.

The northern drives became established as an institution in 1867, when Abilene, on the Kansas Pacific Railroad (then making desultory progress westward) achieved a "cow-town consciousness," and despatched "press-agents" south to urge the advantages of taking herds to Abilene. This year marked the beginning of organized and extensive trail-driving, with the isolated drives in 1866 of Goodnight and Loving, Jim Daugherty, George Duffield, and earlier pioneer drives, fading for the most part into a vague tradition.

When by 1885 Nebraska, Colorado, and Kansas had enacted laws prohibiting the transportation across their borders of Southern cattle, there came the end of the great drives—an end foreshadowed in 1880 by the closure of the Chisholm trail, the customary route from the Red River station on the Texas border into Kansas, by "fool hoe-men," who had preempted practically its whole length, and were tearing its hoof-trampled surface into rows of clods. In 1884 another enemy of the trail, the railroad, successfully invaded the Southwest, and brought thirty thousand cows northward in this first year. But the trail lingered after a fashion until 1895. Ten million cattle and one million horses had been driven its length from Texas to waiting markets; its end was the end of a splendid chapter in the history of the cattle industry, the end of an economic system and the end of the cowboy as a craftsman and gentleman. Thereafter he was merely an employee of "a corporation operating for profit."

Life on the cattle-trails contained much that was wearisome, hard, most unsentimentally tedious. In taking the herds for drives of seventy days or of four months, there were swollen streams to swim, wild runs of cattle that had to be checked by a few men on tired mounts galloping over unknown land, perhaps bandits or Indians to face—the first drives after the Civil War met both—and hardships that lacked even the virtue of the spectacular—drives all day in rain and mud, snatches of sleep on wet ground, sore and useless horses, bad cooking or none at all if brush and chips were wet. Yet men went up the trail year after year, finding work ready for them on the northern ranges at a better wage than Texas cattlemen paid, choosing to go back to Texas and come north with another herd in the next year. Much of the reason lay in an indefinable pride of profession. "A cowboy is not a graduate in his art until he has been up the trail. His education has been sadly neglected if he has never taken a course in this, the highest, branch of the bovine curriculum"—this was the dictum of the trail.

When young Jim Cook asked his boss to make him a trail-hand, the old cattleman replied, "They tell me that you can catch a cow and shoot a rabbit's eye out every pop. Now if you can ride for the next four months without a whole night's sleep, and will turn your gun loose on any damned Indian that tries to steal our horses, why, git ready." And Jim Cook, of course, got ready.

A trail-herd might be directed by the owner himself, or by his straw-boss, the trail-foreman —perhaps by a middleman that might be a "native" known to the cattlemen personally or by reputation, or an outsider whose only recommendation was his money. The elastic code of the Texans of the early days provided differently for each contingency. A buyer of southwest Texas might purchase from his neighbors a herd of 8,000 or 10,000 steers, with no payment at the time of the purchase. The stockowners knew that the buyer needed all the money at his disposal to meet the expenses of the drive; they would not take a note for the purchase price, for honest men dealing with each other needed no notes. The only evidence of debt was the tally of the cattle, giving the numbers in each class, including the mark and the brand they bore. With the other kind of middleman—one instance, cited by Edgar Bronson, will be sufficient: "There was one notorious bit of mixed humor and thrift, when 1200 cattle were converted into 2400, in making the running tally or count, by selecting an isolated hill as the place of their delivery to the monocled, crop-carrying, straight-spurred British buyer, and the simple expedient of running the herd *round* the hill for recount until their actual number was doubled."

The "outfit" that drove the cattle up the trail varied in its numbers with the wealth and wisdom of the owner. There is record of a herd of twenty-five hundred "old mossy-horn steers" driven up the trail in 1876 by twenty-five riders with six head of horses to the man—quite a pageant in view of the outfit of ten men who drove five thousand steers, mostly three-year-olds, a few years later. By 1880 custom suggested that a small herd of eight hundred be taken up the trail by five riders, a herd of fifteen hundred by eight men, and larger herds commensurately.

The first work for the cowboy who had signed to go "up trail" was road-branding. Since a herd might include cattle of several brands, from different owners or from different ranches of the same owner, a common brand—a road-brand—was needed. The work of driving the cattle through a chute and pressing the road-brand on each cow as it was forced through was hard; but anticipations of the drive hurrying the work, the branding went ahead at a lively rate, the mark not burned as deeply as the original brand had been burned. Those cowboys that had been up the trail before subtly boasted of it as they worked by

NEVADA BUCKAROOS

singing some trail ballad, or perhaps a topical adaptation of a familiar song, as:

How dear to my heart are the scenes of my
trailhood,
When fond recollections present them to
view—
The water barrel, the old chuck-wagon,
And the cook who called me to chew.

Once the road-branding was done the herd of perhaps three thousand cattle, with its outfit of sixteen or eighteen cowboys, a cook and his wagon, and a horse-wrangler with the *remuda,* was started northward; if the branding were continued until late in the afternoon, the cattle were allowed to rest until the next dawn. Then, once the cook's call of "Grub pile!" had been answered and the men had saddled their mounts, the drive began. The herd was "drifted" with very little pushing, grazing as it went. By nine o'clock or a little later the men urged the cattle closer together; two riders at each side "pointed" the lead steers at a smart pace, and "swing riders" behind them pushed in the flanks of the herd. Just behind the cattle rode the "tail riders" to keep in the lame and the recalcitrant. "Riding tail" was the least desirable position; these trail-men rode in clouds of dust tossed up by the moving herd, and bore the full brunt of the heat and the smell. The cattle just before them were lame or stupid; those "on the point" had taken the lead of the herd apparently as a recognition of their own importance, and were the least timid and the best physically of the herd.

With the approach of noon, the attention of the cattle turned again to the grass about them, and the swing-riders had to keep in a constant gallop to hold the cows from turning out to graze on the margin of the trail. The cook and the boss went ahead to locate the noon camp, some spot about half a mile from the trail so that the cattle should have fresh grass for the hour's grazing; and by the time the herd came up to the camp, the flap-board on the chuck-wagon had been let down, and a cold lunch was ready for the trail-drivers.

The men smoked and exchanged comments on those cows whose appearance or behavior had made them conspicuous. The cowboy's quick eyes noted and catalogued the individualities of cattle, simply as a mental habit. This keen, almost subconscious detailing of the life about them was a characteristic of frontiersmen. The contribution of the cowboys was an idiom rich with brevities of description, and in these moments when the herd was grazing they spoke with a vivid terseness of cattle and horses and men. Once a few of the cows began to lie down to chew their cuds, the boss knew that they had grazed enough, and gave the signal to resume the drive.

A system of signals came early into use on the trail. The signals were largely borrowed from the plains Indians; they were made principally with the hat, held in the left hand, while the right held the reins. The movement to break camp and move up the trail was simply a wave of the hat in the direction to be taken, made first by the boss, then passed by the line-riders by the point-men. The signal to graze the cattle was again a wave of the hat, toward the side of the trail on which the herd was to be rested.

The morning's drive of six to ten miles might be bettered in the afternoon. The length of this drive was closely related to the distance to water. If the afternoon wore on and there was no sign of water, the cattle would become restless and ill-tempered; but with the first smell of water the lead-cattle, always the most acute, began to bellow, and quickened their pace. "Their necks were stretched and mouths open with continual bawling. It looks like a walking-race; they shuffle along with the most busy determination, careless of aught but the getting over the ground." At last, when the river-bank was reached, the lead steers rushed in till water was halfway up their flanks, and began to drink. The rest followed, spreading out at the bank, going in to drink, and wallow, and stand in placid satiation.

"I have met but few men who knew how to water cattle properly," writes an old cattleman. There was danger that the body of the herd might pour in a mass upon the front cattle, forming a close-trampling pack forcing down the river bottom, sending some frightened cows out to drown in the current, crushing others into the mud; danger of running the cattle into a bank of quicksand; and danger of permitting them to stand still in the water until some became bogged and had to be pulled out by ropes in a slow and often ineffectual process, or be deserted.

Crossing a herd over a flooded stream, muddy and running with a swift current, was a situation escaped only by the trail-drivers of the late summer. The lead-cattle instinctively feared such water, and the point-riders had hard work in urging them on. Sometimes these riders would force their own horses out into the stream to convince the cattle that there was no danger. Once the cattle were out to their swimming depth, they usually went on to the opposite bank with the rest of the herd following. But if a piece of driftwood struck against a steer, or if the leaders became alarmed at the swiftness of the current, the cattle might "mill" in a panic-stricken circle, becoming a confused, struggling mass as other cattle followed. Then came crucial labors for the trail-men; the cattle on the bank had to be checked, and a point-rider had to force his mount into the midst of the frightened mass, break the mill, and force some of the cattle to lead off in swimming for the shore.

Charles Siringo writes of finding the "Salt Fork," near the Kansas line, "bank full and still rising. It was at least half a mile to the opposite side and drift wood was coming down at a terrible rate, which made it dangerous to cross." But the attempt was made; "the old lead steers went right into the foaming water without a bit of trouble and of course the balance followed." The horse of one of the point-riders sank, frightening the lead cattle, and the whole herd turned back in terrible confusion. "Suffice it to say, we remained there seven days without anything to eat except fresh meat without salt. It rained during the whole time nearly, so that we didn't get much sleep on account of having to stay with the cattle night and day."

The classic item in the story of stream-crossing is the entry for June 23, 1866, in the journal of George Duffield: "worked all day in the River trying to make the Beeves swim and did not get one over. Had to go back to Prairie Sick and discouraged. Have *not* got the *Blues* but am in *Hel of a fix.*"

The cattle, once again on the trail, were paced until about sunset, "bedding" time. The boss slowly waved his hat about his head in a circle, and the herd was moved off the trail to its bed ground. The first of the four watches of the night took its place; and the other men gathered about the cook's campfire, to eat generously of a hot supper.

As each of the night-herders rode his arc of the circle of the resting herd, the slow, deep-sounded notes of old songs—"My Bonnie Lies Over the Ocean." "When You and I Were Young, Maggie," and various cloyingly sweet songs that permitted a soothing prolongation of each note—or of the cowboy ballads ("Sam Bass," "The Cowboy's Dream," "The Dying Cowboy," were probably the most popular) quieted the cattle and helped the herder to stay awake. A rider did not dare let drowsiness overtake him; the vagaries of cattle were beyond anticipation, and sleeping on herd duty was unpardonable, meriting instant dismissal. "There was a limit to the endurance of even a rough rider," wrote Jim Cook. "I have been so close to that limit that on one or two occasions I would get a little piece of chewing tobacco from one of the men and, mixing it with saliva, would rub it on my eyelids. This is great treatment when the thoughts seem to be bent on having a nap."

For the cattle did not always lie quietly, getting on their feet only at midnight, for a few moments' exchange of lowing before they lay down again; but startled by some trifle, the sound of a breaking bunch of dry weeds, the cough of a horse, the restiveness of some cow in the herd, perhaps with no cause that the cowboys ever discovered, the whole herd might rise in an uncontrollable torrent. Once frightened, the herd seemed to rise as a unit, rushing away in a frantic mass, perhaps with little bluish flames, from the friction of their bodies, playing at the tips of their horns.

With the first sounds of the stampede each cowboy awoke, mounted the horse he had staked near him, and rode out to help the night-herders in the attempt to break the flight. "It is beef against horseflesh, with the odds on the beef for the first hundred yards." Here was dangerous work for the trail-men. The situation called for a dashing, swearing daredevil, with a horse unafraid to gallop in the dark over unknown country, as eager to end the stampede as his rider.

"The thing to be done is to outrun the herd, neck or nothing." Once up with the leaders of the cattle, the attempt was made to swing them about, by pressing against a leader and using the quirt, or by firing his revolver to the front and on one side of the leaders, a lively pony perhaps aiding by nipping at the hides of the cattle. The cowboys continued to force the swerve until the cattle were milling about in a great circle, round and round in a compact mass. To stop the ineffectual churning and to guard against another wild rush by the cattle trembling but still alert, the cowboys would sing in unison some familiar ballad, or sound that old call of the Texans, which began with "Whoop!" and continued with variations that might have been adapted from a Comanche war-yell. A tenderfoot would have wondered to see cowboys riding about cutting back cattle that were trying to escape from the mill, and to hear them celebrating in chorus the exploits of some train-robber who seemed idiotically irrelevant:

Sam used to deal in race-stock, once called the Denton mare,
He matched her in scrub races, and took her to the Fair.
Sam used to coin the money and spent it just as free.
He always drank good whisky wherever he might be.

After the stampede came a hasty inventory. The stumble of a horse, a sudden swerve of the stampeding cattle, might crush to death a cowboy and his horse; cattle might rush over a bluff or off a steep river-bank, killing some and crippling others of their number in the "pile-up." A stumbling steer would be trampled on by those behind him; some might be gored by the long horns of those they brushed against; legs might be broken and hoofs crushed in the turmoil. If the riders failed to check the herd and hold it in a mass it might become widely scattered, demanding a delay of days while the remnants were gathered. Duffield had worked to the limit of endurance, and uselessly, when he wrote, "Hard run & Wind Big stampede and here we are among the Indians with 150 head of cattle gone—hunted all day & the Rain pouring down with but poor success Dark days are these to me Nothing but Bread and Coffee Hands all Growling & Swearing—everything wet & cold Beeves gone. . . . "

The cause of a stampede was often subtle and unpredictable. One herd that had come from the old King ranch, in south Texas, and had become accustomed to a Mexican cook on the drive to Dodge City, left with a new outfit for a Dakota Indian agency. Once this herd "got wind" of the new cook, a negro, it "made a jump off the bed ground" and attempted to stampede.

A "loony" steer in a herd might keep the rest incessantly nervous. One of John Chisum's herds that seemed to have the habit of stampeding was met on the road by its owner; he ordered the cattle bedded for the night, and rode through the herd for a few minutes, when he pointed out the cause of the stampedes—a one-eyed steer, with wide and crooked horns. The steer was cut out, driven away, and shot; there were no more stampedes on that trip.

Again, a cowboy's carelessness might be the cause. Young Jim Cook, riding about a bedded herd, noticed an old black cow apart from the others; each time as he came around he tried to see how near to that cow he could ride, and after several times around he touched the cow with his foot. With a bound and a snort the cow rose and plunged away—and the stampede was on. Once Robert Wright, riding with an ox-team drive, hung his red and yellow coat over a gentle steer in the "cavayado" of oxen—the rest of the cattle took flight in one of the most devastating stampedes of the sixties. Wright suggested that a wolf had frightened the cattle, and the boss believed him; but some twenty wagons had been completely wrecked, one man's leg and another's arm had been broken, and most of the men were badly bruised.

A storm was almost certain to cause a stampede. Cattle drifted before a strong rain or a wind; all the men could do was to stay with them and sing to them. When lightning and thunder began it was almost impossible to hold all the cattle; with luck most of the herd might be held in a drifting mass. George Scott remembers a night when thirteen steers were killed by lightning and the rest of the herd stampeded in all directions, through creeks and over fences.

Danger of Indian attacks on the trail-herds passed after the first few years of the great drives; the Indian bugaboo died more slowly. In 1878 the Northern Cherokees attempted an outbreak, the last defiant gesture of the Indians on the Territory; but thirteen years later the grangers still feared that parties of marauding Indian bucks might descend on their homesteads in all the glories of war. In this year Captain Bill McDonald of the Texas Rangers traced an Indian scare that gained wide credence to a granger who had heard the revels of a group of cowboys that killed a beef and as they were roasting it capered about the fire and shot their revolvers as a prodigal diversion.

An old Kansas newspaper man has suggested that the cattlemen annually manufactured an Indian scare, if a legitimate one was not forthcoming, to discourage the immigration of "nesters" who were closing the open range of the great herds. Surely it was not the cowboy of the late seventies and the eighties who feared the Indian. "The noble red man never loses anything by neglecting to ask for it," was a range aphorism. The cowboy knew "Lo" as "a lazy, dirty, thieving beggar, who has no business at all on the face of the earth." In the time when Indians in the Territory—those on the Cherokee strip were the worst—might stampede a herd and cause great loss of beef, they could be appeased by the gift of a few aged, footsore steers, or a stray yearling or two. One trail-driver relates with gusto how an Indian chief, old Yellow-Bear came to his camp and demanded bread. The driver told the cook not to give him any, and the red man in his wrath stamped his foot down in a pan of dough the cook was working, and stalked away.

The work of the buffalo-hunters, that ended in the early seventies, had made the northern Indians pitiable when the cowboys came to know them. In 1877 a trail-herd ran afoul of the whole Cheyenne tribe, close to the border of the Territory. "They were half starved, all the buffalo having drifted south, and their ponies were too poor and weak to follow them up. We traded them out of lots of blankets, trinkets, etc. For a pint of flour or coffee they would give their whole soul—and body thrown in for good measure. We soon ran out of chuck too, having swapped it all off to the hungry devils."

For the first few years after the Civil War Indian murders and thefts were a tragic menace to trail-driving. The story of the killing of the pioneer cattleman, Oliver Loving, in 1867, when he was surrounded by Comanches as he rode up the Pecos, is one that for the honest, unwhimpering courage of Loving and the cool fidelity of his companion, Bill Wilson, found two days later and nursed back to health, deserves to live in the straightforward narrative of Frederick Bechdolt. In those days vigilance night and day, with good fortune, was the price of crossing intact a herd through the Indian Territory.

Writes an old trail-driver, "The Indians would sometimes come into camp and beg from us, demanding fat beeves, but we always managed to pacify them. But the grangers displayed a degree of animosity toward the trail-drivers that was almost unbearable."

The gradual change from the old system of open ranges to a system of surveys, deeds, and fences, caught the trail, twisted it, flung it westward, and finally swallowed it. A trail-boss complained in 1884, "Now there is so much land taken up and fenced in that the trail for most of the way is little better than a crooked lane, and we have hard lines trying to find enough range to feed on. These fellows from Ohio, Indiana, and other northern and western states—the 'bone and sinew,' as politicians call them—have made farms, enclosed pastures, and fenced in water-holes till you can't rest; and I say, damn such bone and sinew!" But the cause of a free range and an open drive northward was already lost. When in 1874 the trail-drivers first found watering-places fenced in with barbed wire, they forced the herds through, furious at such malevolent devices. There would have been more "bloody chapters" in cattle-range history if the "fool hoe-men" had dared to open fire on these notoriously accurate gunmen, the cowboys. Many a homesteader's dog "sicked" on the cattle was shot into fragments by the trail-drivers. Kansas jayhawkers who attempted to charge toll on herds crossing their ranges found themselves outdone in sharp practices by the trail-drivers, who issued worthless checks or used open force; but the grangers won the long struggle by sheer force of numbers—by the irrevocable march of civilization, as the platitude runs.

The cattle-drives now, to the nearest railroad siding or from one ranch to another as owners change, are feebly reminiscent of the great drives from as far south as Cameron County, Texas, on the Rio Grande, into Kansas, and perhaps on into the northwest country to stock new ranges. And with the ardors and the importance of the trail no longer present to affect cowboy character, it is easier to understand why the cowboy of to-day prefers phonograph records made in New Jersey to the old songs of the cattle-trail.

CHAPTER SIX

RANCH LIFE

IN the North the ranch-house was usually a large building, the timbers well chinked, perhaps hewn and squared. The windows and the door were carefully fitted, for the cold of winter was sure to find out every gaping joint. Inside was one large unpartitioned room. Cowboys' bunks lined the walls; where they ended began rows of pegs, for the saddles, spurs, bridles, chaps, lariats, and other gear, to be used by those cowpunchers who remembered not to throw their things on the floor. A huge fireplace and a good sized stove were in the room; if on a still summer's night the flavor of ancient bacon-grease might linger in the bunks, in winter the warmth of the cook's fire was a comfort that atoned. In the South, where the warmth of nature was itself sufficient, the cook's house was often a connecting building.

Reginald Aldridge remembers a unique ranch-house he shared with his partner-cattleman in Kansas, where lumber was scarce—a small wooden house, ten feet by six, which could be placed upon an ordinary set of wagon-wheels and drawn about where it was wanted. At one end were the bunks, one over the other; on another side hung a flap-board on hinges, that could be propped up for a table. This portable headquarters was probably better to live in than the little ranch-houses of the small stockmen in the country about Denver, poorly-jointed log affairs that the owners apologized for year after year as only temporary structures.

Simple equipment in ranch-houses was the rule. One long table, near the stove for the convenience of the cook as he dished out the meals, and a few chairs, were enough; perhaps there was also a small table used for card games. "We had lots of wood, a good supply of grub, a keg of whiskey, lots of robes, and one bed," writes John Clay of one of his first camps. This simplicity was as it should be; the range knew instances where the feminine touch, with a Montgomery Ward catalogue to inspire it, had added ornamentation saddening and devastating.

With the beginning of dawn "Miss Sally," the cook, was out of his bunk, grunted to rouse the horse-wrangler, and growled to encourage the coffee. As a coyote, emitting his last wail of the night, trotted off along the horizon line, and "near by in the cottonwoods, a mourning dove called softly to its mate, and from a fence-post a meadow-lark gave full voice in his glad, joyful way," the cowboy came out from his blankets for the morning's coffee and bacon.

The first faint smoke from the stove-chimney had warned the horses grazing outside the ranch-house that the working-day was about to begin; but by the time breakfast was over the horse-wrangler had the skittish herd shut in the corral, ready for the cowboys to pick the mounts they wanted for the day's riding.

Said Roosevelt of his outfit, "We worked under the scorching midsummer sun, when the wide plains simmered and wavered in the heat; and we knew the freezing misery of riding night-guard round the cattle in the late fall roundup. . . . We knew toil and hardship and hunger and thirst, and we saw men die violent deaths as they worked among the horses and cattle, or fought in evil feuds with one another; but we felt the beat of hardy life in our veins, and ours was the glory of work and the joy of living."

The season's routine of "outriding," of making "sign camps," of horse-gentling, of brand-

ON ROUNDUP IN THE ROUGH COUNTRY

ing, needed men who lived and worked in the open by their own choice, who coupled cowcraft and horsemanship with a faithfulness of work that carried them through gamuts of physical ordeals. These men saw life romantically—a wild, free existence, from the morning cup of bitter, pleasant coffee to the night's rest under clear skies.

Groups of cowboys rode on inspection trips, "outridings," to locate the scattered groups of cattle, to note the condition of grass and water, to move back cattle found wandering too near the borders of the range, to watch for danger-signs of men or wolves, to attend to the many details that arose naturally in the course of a season's cow-punching.

A party might discover a yearling with smooth sides and unmarked ears. To rope and brand him might provide some fun, for if the first lariat fell short, the yearling was away at his best pace. Once a rope was tight about the yearling's neck, the rider kept the rope taut while the animal bawled and jumped; but shortly a fire had been built, an iron was taken from its rawhide fastenings on the side of a saddle, and the yearling was branded. If the outriding group found a "maverick" steer, an old "mossback," one or two of the group would ride in pursuit. Once he was roped one or two cowboys dismounted and fastened the steer's feet with a "hog-tie" hitch. If there were no pieces of hobble-rope in the party, the steer might be tied down with his own tail, the hair divided into equal parts and knotted together at the ends, the loop stretched once or twice around the upper hind leg of the steer, keeping that leg drawn up so that the cow could not rise. In the handling of these animals the punchers seemed brave to recklessness. The artist Remington, well acquainted with the West though he was, marveled at the cowboys' "seeming to pay no attention to the imminent possibilities of a trip to the moon . . . . They toss their ropes and catch the bull's feet, they skilfully avoid his rush, and in a spirit of bravado they touch his horns, pat him on the back, or twist his tail." But the appearance of bravado was largely for the entertainment of spectators; behind their studied indifference was the knowledge of cows and their behavior included in the equipment of a genuine cowboy.

"Sign camps" were occasionally established about an entire range. There were two men to each camp; their work was to herd back all cattle that might have drifted across the "line."

The ride of each man was from his "sign camp" half-way toward the next camp. The rides were generally timed so that at the half-way point two riders met, exchanged greetings, and rode back each to his own camp. In the morning the line-riders would search for the trail of any cattle that might have crossed the range boundary during the night; such cattle had seldom wandered far, and were quickly overtaken and driven back. "Starting west of the Utah line, 'most all riding is done from camps, and very seldom is there a change of horses in one day," writes Will James. "There's no night guard, only maybe three or four nights a year, and that's when the cattle is took to the railroad."

"Style" in cowpunching varied with the locality. In the Far Western states the traditions in methods and outfitting that held from Texas to Montana did not always hold, with Mexican labor more common and the roughness of the country demanding different tactics. Texas tradition insisted that one end of the lariat should be tied to the saddle-horn, so that once roped an animal could not escape; a fine rawhide or hemp rope was costly, and an unlucky cowboy sorrowed to see forty feet of lariat trailing after a steer loping toward the horizon.

But in the Far West the rope was "dallied," turned one or two times about the saddle-horn, so that if the roped animal should tumble into a gulch, or attempt to "wind up" the horse and rider, the rope could be turned loose. A cowboy on the northern range rose in his stirrups as he rode a high-tempered horse, while a cowboy farther West "rode close," bobbing up and down with his mount.

Breezy and pleasant days there were on the range, when the cowboy mused as he rode on "the breadth of things, the height of things, the magnificent distances," how fine a country was the West, how fortunate he was to be a part of it.

But there were summer days when the yellow plains were shimmering with heat, when the water the cowboys drank, the ground they slept on, the leather of their saddles were all comfortless and warm. The horses' bits had to be steeped in water before they were adjusted, or the iron would blister the flesh it touched. The water-starved ground, with its gaping cracks, was treacherous footing for haggard, restive cattle. When relief came after such a drouth it was usually a sharp, sudden rainstorm, with vicious flashings of lightning. A veteran cowboy has described his first Kansas storm: "The lightning would strike the ground and set the grass on fire, then the rain would put it out. I got off my horse . . . took off my spurs, six-shooter and pocket knife, laid them down and moved away."

"Some day, as the cowpuncher is riding his rounds about the range, his quick eye may note out on the horizon a faint cloud which has not the appearance of a dust trail. . . . The little cloud does not pass away or grow less, but widens and rises, and all at once fans out on the wind, taking on the unmistakable blue of smoke. There is fire!" The cowboy did not stop to find how the fire had been started; there was work to be done. That crawling line of fire was robbing the cattle of their grass, and bringing ruin to the range.

In the spring of 1876 a great prairie fire was driven from the Staked Plains in the Panhandle into the Canadian River breaks. The fire was sighted at headquarters of the LX ranch late in the evening; saddle ponies were rounded up and dozens of cowboys set out at a swift gallop. A ride of about fifteen miles over rough country in darkness relieved only by the flames brought the party to the fire. Droves of cattle were running ahead of the advancing flames. Some of the largest animals were killed, and their carcasses split open. Then the cowboys paired off, two fastening their ropes to the hind legs of the dead animal, and dragging it to the blaze. If the fire was at the moment burning in an arroyo, where the blue-stem grass grew tall, it was allowed to burn its way to a flat covered with buffalo grass. Here the two cowboys would "straddle the blaze"—one on the burnt side, close up, and the other in the path of the smoke, with his rope played out to its knot on the saddle-horn. The wet carcass was dragged slowly along the line of the blaze, until the carcass was worn into ribbons; then another animal was killed and dragged in its place. What little spots of fire survived were thrashed out by cowboys who followed with pieces of wet cow-hide or with wet saddle-blankets. With only hastily broiled beef to eat in snatches, the cowboys worked on until three o'clock the following evening, when the fire was beaten, and the LX range was saved.

Fire-fighting was a common experience with the ranchman of the West. In Colorado and in Wyoming, where range fires were of seasonal occurrence, the ranchmen kept wet green hides ready when the outbreak of fire seemed likely. "It must be a bad fire if the cowboys do not check it," writes Hough, "for they rush into the work with all that personal carelessness of fatigue or danger which marks them in all their work and so labor as long as they can sit in their saddles, sometimes coming out of the smoke with eyebrows singed off, hands blistered, and faces black and grimed, their eyes small and red from the glare and heat of the battle with this enemy of the range. When they are through with the fight they sleep, eat, and vow revenge."

As winter came ranch outfits were reduced, and the cattle-country knew quieter months. But if the assignments were fewer, the cowboys' work was more strenuous. The cattle had to be guarded; and out-riding and night-herding in the biting cold, however unpleasant, had to be done. Ropes and saddle-blankets sometimes were stiff and icy, and cowboys "rose and froze all day and some more of it on night guard."

On large ranches some cowboys were detailed to live through the winter at line camps, two or four cowboys to each outfit.

The cattle split up into bunches, each taking possession of some small valley or slope where a spring or a creek was near. But with the coming of a heavy snow the cattle were guided by line-riders to where the grass was plentiful and the snow above it not too deep. Unlike horses, cattle could not eat snow, nor did their instinct suggest that they paw away the snow to reach the grass beneath. Cattle have been known to sustain themselves by following a herd of horses, drinking the melted snow gathered in the hoof prints, and nibbling the grass that had been exposed.

If an ice crust formed over the snow, the range suffered. Live stock could not eat grass-blades coated with ice; and if horses could not paw through the ice-sheet, the stock was helpless. While these conditions continued, cowboys had to ride through the herds to keep weak cattle from lying on the ground until they became too stiff and cramped to rise. The cowboys had to "tail 'em up"—to twist the tail of the benumbed animal until the agony forced it to rise. "Tailin' up" was an ungrateful task; the steer, maddened by the pain, often rushed angrily toward the mounted cowboy, perhaps to lose his footing and stumble again helpless on the snow.

Cattle were sure to drift in the course of a winter. With the grass buried deep under the snow, the herd would suddenly begin to drift in a body, marching in some direction that might lead them to grass and water. The drift might be for miles, until the herd encountered a hill, a cliff, or some other barrier; then the march backward would begin, the cattle browsing in the swath they had cut in the snow.

But in a storm the drift might not end so harmlessly. Under a biting wind and a thick fall of snowflakes cattle have started to drift with the wind, each animal going on until it was too weak to stand; and once it dropped it was only "fit for the coyotes." Before impassable obstacles the cattle have huddled in hopeless masses; there were years when against the fences on either side of the Santa Fe track the carcasses of drifted cattle have formed lines unbroken for miles.

If storms were few and slight, winter on the range passed rather pleasantly for the cowboys. Within the ranch-house at night, an old-timer relates, "We used to pile up the blazing logs, sing songs, and forget the weather outside. I cannot say that there was any great musical talent displayed, but the performers enjoyed these extempore concerts, and there was no audience to criticise."

Standard brands of canned tomatoes, condensed milk, and tobacco were used throughout the cow-country; out of familiarity with these cans and sacks the cowboy came to know, almost without effort, the wording of the labels; sometimes the cowboys gathered in a ranch-house repeated the legends in unison, as an aimless pastime. The zest of these memory-tests might be heightened by levying cash penalties for mistakes.

And there was always poker. The stock-owners played the cards "clear to the roof," and the cowboys were too fond of the game to confine their bets to cash on hand. Spurs, extra saddle-blankets, extra shirts, almost anything would be wagered in the excitement of "deuces wild."

During the winter occasional dances were held at the larger ranches and in the frontier towns. Formal dress included the cowboy's guns—the rest was left to his personal taste. Broad-brimmed hats, jingling spurs, and chaps—many a cowboy wore all these on the floor; but the Beau Brummels removed these adornments with their "extra clothes" that had been needed for the ride of many miles to the scene of the dance. Pants were commonly kept tucked into boot-tops.

A fiddle or two supplied the music; pianos were rare in the range country. Beside the "orchestra" stood the master of ceremonies, who directed the dances almost as he pleased. "Now then, gentlemen," his call would ring out, and bottles would be replaced hastily in hip pockets, "get your pardners on the floor." He might announce a "quordreele," a "shorteesche," a "glide polka," or a "set." If it were a set, he ordered the figures at his own fancy—a "chassez," a gallopade, *dos-à-dos,* reversé, or another of the several complicated movements the cowboys knew—

Gents to center, ladies 'round 'em,
Form a basket, balance all!
Whirl your gals to where you found 'em
Promenade around the hall!
Balance to yer pards and trot 'em,
'Round the circle double quick,
Grab an' kiss 'em while you've got 'em,
Hold 'em to it if they kick.

But there were not enough to be grabbed and kissed for general satisfaction. There were nearly always ten to six men for each lady. "It was always a wonder to me," one cowboy has mused, "how the supposed to be weaker sex could tire the men even at that, but they did, and the fatter they was the longer they stayed."

Midnight usually marked an intermission,

with a big feed of half a dozen kinds of cake and as much steaming coffee as the cowboys could drink. Once these moments of rest were over, the fiddler resumed his post, and the dance continued until daybreak. "The ladies all disappeared then, and us boys would take the floor and go on with the stag dance; if 'fire-water' was around that stag dance was apt to be kind of tough and end up in wrestling matches."

Breakfast was spread; and after the coffee there was talk of hitting the trail, and soon, "with a lot of howdedo," the cowboys of each ranch started over the snow on the ride home.

Almost every ranch had its cowboy musician; and in evenings the cowboys sometimes listened to those same tunes that served for the square dances—"Cotton Eyed Joe," "Old Dan Tucker," "Black Jack Grove," "Hogs in the Cornfield," "The Old Gray Mare Came Tearing Through the Wilderness."

The dance and the dance-music harkened back to a small-town society that many cowboys had once known. There were not many of these social contacts in the cowboy's life. Ranch mails were always small, no matter how large the outfit or how infrequent their arrival. Edgar Bronson wrote of his fellow-cowboys,

"For most of them such was the rarity of letters that often have I seen a cowboy turning and studying an unopened envelope for a half-day or more, wondering whoever it was from and guessing whatever its contents might be."

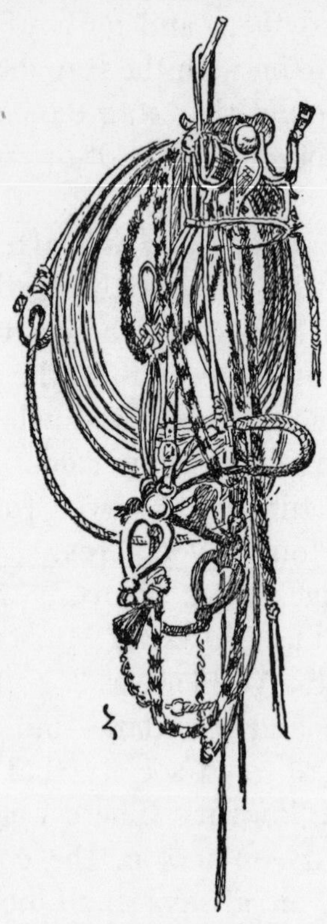

RIDING TOOLS—REATA, HACKAMORE, BRIDLE AND SPURS

CHAPTER SEVEN

THE WESTERN RANGE

WINTER came early in 1866, and somewhere on the plains of western Nebraska two bullock trains engaged in freighting goods from the Missouri to points in the Rockies were halted by heavy snows. The bosses gave up hope of completing the drive; they cached their wagons, turned the oxen loose, and rode back to report their failure to Alexander Majors and the Wells-Fargo agents. In the spring they returned to the abandoned train, driving oxen before them to replace those that had been left to die in the ravages of the winter; but instead of bleached skeletons they found the oxen themselves, sleek and contented. This accident furnished evidence that cattle could live and thrive throughout the year on the northern plains, and the open range was soon after extended from the Southwest into a new and greater cattle country.

As the decade of the seventies opened, the

wholesale killing of the buffalo was drawing to a close, the profession of buffalo-hunting becoming increasingly precarious as the herds were diminished; the menace of roving Indians was too slight to frighten armed cowboys; and railroads in their westward advance were bringing the cattle market nearer. In May, 1869, the Union Pacific and the Central Pacific had met to form an unbroken line to the Pacific coast; the Kansas Pacific had reached Denver, and in 1870 was finished a connecting link with the Union Pacific, a road from Denver to Cheyenne. Into the plains country and the ranges to the north of the railroads came the cattlemen. "Immediately in the wake of the buffalo hunter came the cowboy; and following the buffalo came the long-horned steer."

In these days of the first invasion it seemed all a golden land. There was surely in these limitless expanses room for all the cattle that scores of years would bring. Great herds, the foundations of great fortunes, were quickly established. Shorthorn cattle, Kentucky the great source of supply, were brought into the ranges to modify the old angular, thin-girthed Longhorn stock.

By the law of the range the newcomers had first rights. The grass was to be free to the cattleman who actually occupied the range. As in Texas, agreements concerning the partitioning of the range and the use of water became property rights, and were frequently bought and sold. Such a system could be based only on a general respect for a man's rights once they were determined; there was no law to adjust questions of title, and the cattleman wanted none. For the privilege of managing his business with a free hand, he was willing to protect his own property without assistance from the law.

For years cattle were dealt in by thousands, on contracts which were simply verbal agreements; or if the formalities of business were to be observed, a few figures might be penciled on the back of a tomato-can label. Buying by "book count" was the common method. Gathering and rebranding to determine the exact number of cattle in a herd was a time-wasting, costly process. "It is safe to say that in many cases not half of the cattle represented on the books were in actual existence," writes an old cattleman. "The owners were honest but the wastage was far greater than any of us expected." But in the fervor of speculation, book counts were the basis of transactions, and were accepted as security by the banks. It was an era of optimism and honesty; in the words of a loan agent, "It is fair to say that in those early years we never had a wilful misrepresentation, a single dirty act such as a mean debtor can play up against you."

In 1870 three hundred thousand Texas cattle were driven up the trail into Kansas; about half of these were stock-cattle to sell to the northern range-men. The beeves to be sent to Eastern markets found eager buyers, for prices were high, and in the terrific price-war between the trunk-line railroads from Chicago to the Atlantic seaboard freight charges had been cut almost to nothing.

This boom year had its inevitable consequence. In the fall of 1871 the plains of Kansas were stocked with cattle by newcomers who had read that a start with five or eight hundred cattle in this western country, where grass and water were as free as the air, would bring tremendous wealth in four or five years. There was not one of these men who rode the Kansas plains that autumn who did not believe that his fortune was made; the height the prairie grass would surely be by the first of March was measured on table-legs as men met to exchange gossip on prices and markets. The Kansas winters were so mild, it was said, that there was hardly any need for coats; and some enthusiasts cited statistics to show that an increase of population in a region brought about an increase in the rainfall.

And when the terrible winter was over, the owners rode out from their snowbound ranch-houses, and found a half, perhaps a fourth, of their cattle still alive.

The story of the cattle-country for the next few years is largely a repetition of the story of these two, with boom times bringing overspeculation and overstocking, to be followed by a devastating winter or a crash in the market. But the influx of cattlemen and cattle continued. Montana and Arizona alike were occupied. Englishmen sought out the plateaus of Colorado, and Americans learned of a new cattle-raising country through English newspapers and magazines. Then from the overcrowded East began an exodus of young men, many collegians among them. Wrote a cultured correspondent from Colorado in 1882, "It may safely be said that nine-tenths of those engaged in the Far West are gentlemen."

Before Charlie Siringo quit cow-punching to become a storekeeper, he had seen the tightening of property lines and the passing of the old freedom. "Well do I remember of 'Shanghai' Pierce once riding into our camp, when one of his animals was being butchered, he said, 'Boys, the day is coming when every man will have to eat his own beef.' " There came a new type of boss into this new cattle-country—economical men who gave serious study to cattle and cattle-breeding, and kept ledgers. When Texas cowboys found that to get high wages on the northern ranches "sobriety, self-restraint, and decent behavior" were enjoined on them, they knew that the cattle-country was no longer young. Siringo in 1882 had voiced the attitude of the old-timers from Texas: "Cattle are becoming so tame, from being bred up with short horns, that it requires very little skill and knowledge to be a cowboy. I believe the day is not far distant when cowboys will be armed with prod-poles to punch the cattle out of their way—instead of fire-arms. Messrs. Colt and Winchester will then have to go out of business or else emigrate to 'Arkansaw' and open up prod-pole factories."

As the range became occupied, and contests arose over water-privileges and the richer grazing-areas, the position of the cowboy was profoundly affected. Called upon to assert his clanship, he became one of a military fraternity, holding the interests of his boss against rustlers, sheepmen, grangers, even against other cattlemen.

Much—in fiction and in articles for magazines with a large New England circulation, too much—has been written of the conflicts between sheepmen and cattlemen. A hundred years ago Mexicans held large sheep-ranches in southwest Texas, practically unmolested; but sheep-raising was a small-scale industry, and the great cattleman looked down upon it accordingly. For a herd of three thousand sheep—and most herds were much less—an outfit was complete with a white man, the flockmaster, two Mexican herders under him, and a cook. The drifting herder held his flocks on grazing lands along a stream until after shearing time; then he started out following the grasses until he had meandered back to his old camp or to a marketing-place.

The cowboy despised the sheep-herder, and despised the sheep that in their wanderings nibbled the grass close to the earth and trampled the roots with their sharp hoofs, and left about watering-places an odor that cattle seemed to like as little as did cowboys. Wrote Theodore Roosevelt, cattleman, "We hold in about equal abhorrence the granger who may come in to till the land and the sheep-owner who drives his flocks over it."

With the beginning of this century came the crisis in the struggle for free range between sheepmen and cattlemen. In the nineties "the unwritten law of priority" had been invoked in drawing a dead-line between sheep-range and cattle-range. A Republican tariff was keeping up the price of wool, and cattle were bringing increasingly good prices; there might have been mutual prosperity, with no more open conflict than the unspoken hostilities that had always existed, if "nesters"—irrigationists and dry-farmers—had not preëmpted lands that had seemed destined for grazing only. Sheepmen and cattlemen were forced close together on a smaller range—and warfare followed.

In western Wyoming the sheepmen decided to ignore the dead-line set by the cattlemen. An army of cowboys rode in upon the trespassing sheepmen and ousted one hundred thousand sheep from the cattle-land; the sheepmen's wagons were burned and the herders given warning never to return. When the sheep were again driven into the Green River country the cowboys met them again, clubbed four thousand to death, and drove the rest across the dead-line. Later, at Big Piney, after another invasion of the cattle-country, the sheep-herders were tied to trees and forced to watch the clubbing of their flocks and the burning of their wagons.

The conflict in Colorado was marked by the killing of a sheep-owner, Pete Swanson. Swanson and one herder were about to drive a flock across the dead-line, when a party of cattlemen, all masked, rode up to them. In the spectacular narrative of a writer for *Harper's Weekly,* " 'Swanson, up with your hands. My God! You shan't enter the cow land with that bunch of sheep,' cried the leader. Up went the herder's hands. Like a flash up came Swanson's rifle. 'I'm an American citizen,' said he, spiritedly. 'This is government land. I'll stand to my rights.' One of the riders raised his carbine—Swanson covered him—his gun snapped. A puff of smoke from the riders and 'Pete' Swanson was dead." The herder was tied and gagged; then the party of cattlemen rode among the sheep, bending low and clubbing as they went. In a few minutes the butchery was complete.

In 1907 and again in 1908 sheepmen attempted successfully a mass invasion of the cattle country, on the drive to winter ranges. The cattlemen attempted a few legal prosecutions; and when in January, 1909, these cases were thrown out of court, the cattleman-sheepman conflict came to a long overdue close. The sheepmen had won. On the semiarid ranges, including Federal preserves, sheep dominate.

The rustler, cattle-thief and horse-thief, was in this new cattle-country from its beginning. In Texas rustling had been a casual diversion of a cowboy out of work, often a simple misdemeanor in the eyes of the law. A cowboy might rustle a small herd from a ranch in southwest Texas, drive across the Rio Grande, and sell the herd to some Mexican stockman—theft undignified in its very ease, and without the solace of a good profit. But after the Civil War remnants of the little guerrilla armies, and many regular soldiers left impoverished and discouraged, drifted to the frontier for easy money and a rough life. Some, starting with a few cattle paid for to furnish an appearance of respectability, set about extending their interests—by judiciously careless branding of whatever unmarked stock they could find. Of even more ingenuous morality was that old Confederate captain who settled at Roswell, New Mexico, with the idea that he was practically out of the United States, and proceeded to increase his herd by "mavericking" on a large scale.

The simple process of roping and branding an unmarked cow, a "maverick," was soon supplemented by a complicated technique of brand-blotting and branding, thievery on an audacious, organized basis. This development attended the increase of herds upon the ranges and the outnumbering of Texas bosses and owners by Northerners and foreigners—Englishmen and Scotchmen. For an outfit of thoroughbred Texas cowboys a tenderfoot owner was one to be distrusted and ridiculed; and a tenderfoot foreman was an outright humiliation, his simplest orders a personal affront to these veterans of the range.

As bosses with strange ideas of efficiency and organization, who considered temperance first and ability afterward when they hired their cowboys, became more common on the range, disgruntled and idle cowboys turned to rustling cattle, to "get even." Cowboys who had "gone bad" from cow-town whisky and dance-hall companions drifted to rustling in their hunt for ready money. Some of the big corporations, in attempting to swell their herds at the expense of the small cattlemen, offered a bounty on each "maverick" branded for the home ranch; this brought their cowboys within one step of actual rustling, and many of them crossed the pale. The next "business step" of the big companies was to permit no cowboy to own a brand of his own, and to pay no more commissions on "mavericks." For many this order was the final insult; out-and-out rustling increased a hundredfold. The West, it seemed, was becoming the toy of Eastern capital. The code of the West was being twisted by alien hands; the old loyalties of the cowboy had been broken for him.

Criminals that drifted to the frontier seldom became rustlers; they lacked skill at riding and shooting, they lacked acquaintance with the ways of cattle and knowledge of any number of brands. This knowledge was invaluable in brand-burning; the accomplished rustler knew not only the brands, but the number of cattle and the efficiency or carelessness of the ranches for many miles about his base.

Brand-burning was the altering of brands so that owners, if they found their stolen cattle, had no proof by which they could identify them. Successful manipulation of a straight rod over an old brand required skill, or the flesh might be seared and the alteration revealed. A talented rustler might stretch a wet

RUSTLERS CAUGHT

scrap of an old blanket over the old brand, and rebrand through the blanket to make the alteration less sharp. But the danger of "botching" such a job was great; and a "botched" job was an acute mortification to most rustlers.

In the upper Rio Grande country, just west of the Staked Plains, "the badness of the whole frontier," rustlers, outlaws, and refugees, had crystallized by 1876. The outcome of the meeting of this backwash of the great trail with the ranchers just occupying the range of Lincoln County was the vicious "Lincoln County War," a series of indiscriminate killings that discredited the entire range country as journalists lingered fascinated over the bloody spectacle.

By the middle seventies rustlers infested the ranges of Montana and Wyoming; organized in a loose recognition of kinship, they stole horses and ran off cattle almost as they pleased. These gangs were met by Vigilance Committees and by the stockgrowers' associations. Designed first to protect their members at the central markets and to arrange for systematic roundups, these associations turned naturally to problems of range protection. In 1891 the Wyoming Stock Growers' Association announced, "There has been made public, although it was known to many intimately connected with the range, a system of stealing which in its effects has been not only disastrous to those engaged in the business of cattle raising, but has had a disheartening effect on investors. . . . It is a matter of life or death." But the great stockowners were not able to enlist the small cattlemen in their war against rustlers, because of their high-handed business methods and their practice of hiring men to battle with the rustlers, old buffalo-hunters and ex-cowboys with notched guns, or at worst private detectives, "barroom gladiators," hired to exterminate the rustlers, and ready to make good.

The warfare in Wyoming reached its dénouement in the next year, in the "Johnson County War" of 1892. Rustlers had served notice on the cattlemen that no spring roundups were to be permitted that year, and openly shipped beef in carload lots to the East. In four years the cattlemen brought one hundred and eighty suits against rustlers in Johnson County, securing one conviction—that of a rustler who had killed a cow and taken home a quarter of beef, for which offense he was pronounced guilty of petty larceny and assessed the value of the beef.

Early in the spring the large stockowners met at Cheyenne and planned a general raid against the rustlers. "It was very much an affair of going after rustlers with a brass band," comments Hough. For three weeks special newspapermen wrote a sensational story a day on the affair. Two rustlers were killed, and the War ended in farcical bathos.

Against the granger there could be no effective fighting.

"Nesters," the cattlemen of the Southwest called the cowboys who left the ranch for the farm, "nesting" most likely because of some girl who would not marry a nomadic cowboy. The term was extended to homesteaders and squatters, men whose plots soon dotted expanses where great herds still roamed at large. These small farmers were often alien, sullen, jealous of their little domain, knowing nothing of range freedom and Western open-handedness and caring nothing.

When the big cattleman began fencing his lands, he included great sweeps that might envelop entirely the plots of several nesters. If the nester, shut off from his usual road and perhaps shut off from water, cut down a part of the fence, the next time he came to the gap he might find a cowboy with a Winchester waiting for him. The war was on; and sometimes the nesters strangely found allies among the cowboys themselves, cowboys that hated fences and all they symbolized.

To a ranch where John Clay was stopping there came a family of homesteaders, their horses confused in the storm. Once the cold torrent of rain had stopped, the horses were harnessed to the wagon, to drive on in the bitter weather through the night. No one made a protest against the family's starting. Clay commented discreetly what a shame it was to allow people to leave the ranch in such a night. "Let 'em go," said a cowboy. "They drove us out of Kansas, now let them lie where they made their bed."

If there was a typical attitude among the cowboys toward the grangers, it was a contemptuous tolerance. The cowboys might cut the nesters' fences to let the stock escape, and set about by a hundred petty persecutions to drive a few grangers from a range, but they had no love for such methods. Cowboys were proud of their calling; they were bred to the life, and they loved it. Farmers, mechanics, and tradesmen were drudges, stupid folk, and to be pitied. As the fences spread and the free grass vanished, the cowboy of the Western range knew he was doomed; but he proposed to die like a gentleman. "Ranch life is ephemeral," said Roosevelt over twenty-five years ago. "I, for one, shall be sorry to see it go; for when the cowboy disappears, one of the best and healthiest phases of western life will disappear with him."

CHAPTER EIGHT

AFTER-SUPPER CELEBRITIES

EACH cow carried its own life history in signs burned deep into its hide. If a cow passed its days uneventfully on one ranch until it went under the block or died in happy old age, it bore only one brand, the mark of its one owner. But cattle that passed from ranchman to ranchman were seared with many branding irons, until with the confusion of letters and figures there seemed hardly room for the burrs and mud and yellowed grass-blades that every cow acquired.

Cowboys described the brands in a jargon as incisive as the brands themselves. The last cow at

The roundup we had at Mayou
On the Lightning Rod range, near Cayo

was "read off" by Ol' Nigger Add as

Overslope in right ear an' de underbit,
Lef' ear swaller fork an' de undercrop,

Hole punched in center, an' de jinglebob
Under half crop, an' de slash an' split.

She's got O Block an' Lightnin' Rod,
Nine Forty-Six an' A Bar Eleven,
T Terrapin an' Ninety-Seven,
Rafter Cross an' de Double Prod.

Half Circle A an' Diamond C,
Four Cross L and Three P Z,
B W I, X V V,
Bar N Cross an' A L C.

So if none o' you punchers claims dis cow,
Mr. Stock 'Sociation needn't git 'larmed;
For one more brand more or less won't do no harm,
So old Nigger Add'l just brand her now.

An unbranded cow was called a "maverick." Most of the range terms had been adopted by the first Texas cowboys from the Mexican *vaqueros;* but the word "maverick" carried a story with it. Just what this story was not many cowboys really knew; but all had explanations. About camp fires the story of "Maverick" developed into a folk-tale—a legend with many variations.

A common story was that in the forties or fifties an enterprising Texan by the name of Maverick made a business of searching the range for unbranded cattle and running his own brand upon all that he found; and in memory of what had happened to many unbranded cattle all such stock became known as "mavericks." Some learned cowboy related this shadowy Texan to the Mavericks of Boston. In a part of Colorado the word became "Mauvrick," "from an old Frenchman in Texas who is said to have added largely to his worldly store by a systematic abstraction of these waifs and strays."

A popular explanation spread from Kansas. A Mr. Maverick, according to this story, moved into Texas shortly after the province had become a republic. He was astonished to find every one's stock branded and earmarked, which had not been the custom in his native Southern state. Maverick was "a chicken-hearted old rooster," and thought branding cruel, so he chose to let his cattle run unmarked; they would be known for Maverick's because cattle belonging to any one else would bear a brand. His neighbors soon provided brands for these loose cattle, and in a few years Maverick was a ranchman without stock.

The facts are these: M. A. Maverick, a citizen of San Antonio, left a herd out on the range for another man to tend. But no round-ups were held, no branding-irons were heated, and Maverick's cattle became scattered over the vast range of south Texas. When the cowboys of this section discovered an unbranded cow, they knew that they had probably found a "Maverick," and usually settled the question of ownership by burning their own brand on the animal.

When the talk of cowboys drifted from range customs to range history, the story of the drive of Jim Daugherty in the spring of 1866 was often told. "Uncle Jim" Daugherty himself was one of the best-known Texas cattlemen; and the account was appreciated all the more because the hardships it included had passed early in the history of the trail.

Daugherty started from Denton County with a herd of five hundred steers and an outfit of five cowboys besides himself. He expected to drive to Sedalia, and from there to send the cattle by rail to St. Louis.

At Baxter Springs, Kansas, he learned that jayhawkers had molested the herds ahead of him, and in one instance had killed the owner, driven away the cowboys, and seized the herd.

Under the pretext of fearing the transmission of Texas fever to the native cattle, lawless gangs, jayhawkers, were in this year perpetrating all manner of outrage and robbery. "The practice, "wrote Jim McCoy, "was to go in force and armed to the teeth, surround the drover, insult him by words such as a cowardly bully only knows how to use; spit in his face, snatch handfuls of beard out, tie him to a tree and whip him . . . tie a rope around his neck and choke him. In short, provoke him to a demonstration of resistance . . . then kill him and straightway proceed to appropriate his herd."

After learning of the outrages Daugherty stopped his herd in the Indian Territory, and rode ahead to investigate. At Fort Scott, Kansas, he met Mr. Keyes, a cattle-buyer, who agreed to take the herd if Daugherty made delivery at Fort Scott.

He returned to his herd and pointed the drive along the Kansas-Missouri line. The outfit was on the lookout for trouble, and twenty miles south of Fort Scott it came.

Daugherty and one of his cowboys, John Dobbins, were riding at the head of the herd when fifteen or twenty jayhawkers came upon them. Dobbins attempted to draw his gun, and was instantly shot; the muzzles of a dozen guns were upon Daugherty, and he was forced to surrender. Frightened by the shot, the cattle stampeded; the four cowboys at the rear stayed with the cattle, and succeeded in holding most of the cattle some distance away.

The jayhawkers took their prisoner to a nearby creek, and there amused themselves with a "trial." Daugherty was accused of bringing tick-infested cattle into the country, and, skipping the formality of considering evidence, was found guilty. In his own words, "Some wanted to hang me while others wanted to whip me to death. I, being a young man in my 'teens and my sympathetic talk about being ignorant of ticky cattle of the south diseasing any of the cattle in their country caused one of the big jayhawkers to take my part. The balance were strong for hanging me on the spot but through his arguments finally let me go." The story as cowboys usually told it included a scene in which the jayhawkers tied Daugherty to a tree and lashed him terribly.

"After I was freed and had joined the herd, two of my cowboys and I slipped back and buried John Dobbins where he fell. After we had buried him we cut down a small tree and hewed out a head and footboard and marked his grave. Then we slipped back to the herd." Daugherty found that about one hundred and fifty head had been lost in the stampede.

The herd was driven back into the Indian Territory, and Daugherty went back to Fort Scott to report the attack to his prospective buyer. Mr. Keyes sent a guide who knew the country well to help Daugherty in completing the drive.

The cattle were driven only at night. About daybreak of the fifth night the herd reached Fort Scott, and was driven into a high board corral where it was completely hidden from public view. "As soon as the cattle were penned Mr. Keyes paid me for them. Then we ate our breakfast and slept all day. When darkness fell we saddled our horses and started back over the trail to Texas."

More in the range of ordinary occurrence, more optimistic a tale, was the story of Robert Hunter's drive in 1866. It was such a narrative as cowboys told in turn when conversation strayed to personal experiences.

Like many another cattleman, Hunter was of Scottish birth. His father had settled as a farmer and stockman in Illinois; Hunter himself had been in the Pike's Peak gold rush, had taken a flyer in a quartz milling venture, had followed the reports of fabulously rich mines in Arizona, then had settled in Missouri, where he sold oxen to the freighters who carried goods across the "great American desert" to Army posts and traders' settlements.

At the close of the Civil War, he started to Texas to buy cattle, but before reaching the Red River he met a herd coming north. He bought the entire herd at twenty-five dollars a head, and hired back the trail-drivers to bring the cattle into Missouri.

The western line of Vernon County, Missouri, was passed but a few miles, when "a coon-skin-capped biped calling himself the sheriff of Vernon County" took formal possession of the herd and arrested Hunter, probably on the old scare-cry of transmitting Texas fever to the northern herds. About ten thousand cattle were already in the possession of the sheriff, their owners under arrest.

Early the next morning Hunter told the sheriff that he did not want to go to jail, that he would prefer to make his own living rather than burden the good people of Vernon County with his support; if the sheriff would accompany him to Lamar, the county seat, Hunter could easily find friends to go his bail. The sheriff was reasonable; and the two started on

"THE REP"

the thirty-five mile ride. Once they were out of sight, all the herds were put on the trail, heading directly west for the Indian neutral lands.

At Lamar the genial Hunter invited the "coon-skin-capped biped" into a saloon, and "treated" in a grand fashion. Shortly after Hunter rode away to join his herd, leaving the sheriff floundering in a mud-puddle beside the saloon.

The herds proceeded from the Indian lands into Kansas. Once they were delayed for a few days by German squatters; but Hunter at last reached Bartlett Station, on the Rock Island, and here he shipped his cattle to Illinois, where they were fattened on blue-grass pasture for the Chicago market. Hunter made six thousand dollars on the venture.

The cowboy did not try to find words for his emotions as he gazed from a high mesa into green distances; nor did he break his silence as he listened to the story of Oliver Loving, who challenged horizons, who ignored dangers because he loved life.

In 1858 Loving drove a bunch of cattle from Texas to Illinois; the next year he pushed into the West, taking his herd to winter on the range about Pueblo. In 1866 Loving and

Charlie Goodnight pooled their herds and drove the cattle to Western posts and Indian reservations.

In 1867 the two cattlemen started another herd on the same trail, from the Brazos River to the Pecos and on northwest to Denver. On the Brazos they were joined by Bill Wilson, driving a herd westward. For protection against the Indians, the cattle were thrown together. After days of driving through unfailing rain, Horsehead Crossing on the Pecos was reached; then the three owners decided that Loving and Wilson should ride ahead to Fort Sumner, New Mexico, to secure the contract for furnishing the Indians there with cattle, while Goodnight trailed with the herd. Goodnight knew the dangers of riding through an Indian-infested country and attempted to persuade Loving that only by traveling at night could he hope to reach the fort.

But Loving could not be cautious long; and on the second day the two cowmen, riding boldly by day, sighted a party of Comanches heading towards them from the southwest. Loving and Wilson left the trail and rode toward the Pecos River, four miles to the northwest. They reached the Pecos in time to scramble down its bank and hide among its sand dunes and cane-brakes. There was no chance to save the horses from the Indians. Over a hundred Comanches were in the war party; and in a moment the two fugitives were surrounded on all sides.

In moving from one clump of bushes to another, Loving exposed himself to an Indian's fire; a ball passed through his wrist and entered his side. The shot was the signal for a desperate charge; but Wilson, emptying first his own gun and then Loving's, helped his companion to a sandy hollow where high weeds concealed them both.

"We lay there until night," relates Wilson. "Mr. Loving's wounds had thrown him into a high fever, and I managed to bring up some water from the river in his boot, which seemed to relieve him somewhat. About midnight the moon went down, but the Indians were still around us. We could hear them on all sides. Mr. Loving begged me to leave him and make my escape so I could tell his folks what had become of him. He said he felt sure he could not last until morning and that if I stayed on I would be killed too. He insisted that I take his gun, as it used metallic cartridges and I could carry it through the water and not dampen the powder. Leaving with him all of my pistols and my rifle, I took his gun and with a handclasp told him good-bye."

Wilson stripped to his underclothing—and his hat—and plunged into the river. He was a one-armed man; the gun was a greater weight than he could support, so he pushed the muzzle into the river-bottom and floated downstream, somehow avoiding the notice of the many Comanches along the banks.

When he had floated well out of the trap, he climbed up a bank, through its fringe of cane-brake, and began his three days' march, barefooted, over ground that was a mass of thorny plants. "On my way I picked up the small end of a tepee pole which I used for a walking stick. The last night of this painful journey the wolves followed me all night. I would give out, just like a horse, and lay down in the road and drop off to sleep and when I would awaken the wolves would be all around me, snapping and snarling. I would take up that stick, knock the wolves away, get started again and the wolves would follow behind. I kept that up until daylight, when the wolves quit me. About 12:00 o'clock on the last day I crossed a little mountain and knew the boys ought to be right in there somewhere with the cattle. I found a little place, a sort of cave, that afforded protection from the sun, and I could go no further." Here Charlie Goodnight found him.

When Wilson had recovered sufficiently to tell his story somewhat coherently, Goodnight at once left his herd and rode with his trail-drivers to find Loving. The spot Wilson had described was located, but Loving was not there.

Two weeks later the Texans met a party from Fort Sumner, which brought the news that Loving was at the fort. The night following Wilson's escape he had dragged himself to the river, and had drifted past the Indians. He made his way to the road where it struck the river, and lay there for five days until some Mexicans came by and discovered him. They carried him to the fort; but an untended wound and seven days of starvation were too great odds, and shortly after Goodnight and Wilson reached the fort Loving was dead.

To follow the story of Loving's drive with a narrative like it would have betrayed the sentimental streak in the group of story-tellers and listeners; and if the cook was not growling that he would wake every man in the outfit "early as all hell" in the morning, some one might begin the always-popular story of the great Sam Bass.

Sam Bass was born in Indiana, it was his native home.

And like Jesse and Frank James and Cole and Bob Younger, he was a virtuous youth. In the sweet atmosphere of his Christian home Sam lived quietly, but uncomfortably, until at fourteen he became an orphan. At once he gave up going to church and Sunday school; he started chewing Kentucky leaf and experimenting in profane language. At seventeen or eighteen, he ran away. He came south by steamer, and found work in a Mississippi sawmill. Here, it seems, he rapidly became expert at "card playing, dissipation, and revolver shooting."

In 1870 Sam Bass came to Denton, Texas, and became a cowboy. After a year of the life, he was made a deputy sheriff. Sam was the owner of a fast sorrel mare; the winnings of his races kept him in whisky. Resigning his star by request, he devoted himself to horse-racing and high living.

When his sorrel mare had become too famous in Denton County for Sam to make further matches, he and two companions went north into the Indian Territory, taking with them a string of horses to bet against the best of the Indians' mounts. But the races that were to bring the wealth of the Cherokees and Choctaws into the pockets of the three adventurers ended sadly; their string was wagered and lost, and the trio waded back into Texas.

That night Sam Bass graduated from gambling and tobacco-chawing to horse-stealing. While the Indians slept, the three friends recrossed the river, and drove into Texas their own horses and many that had belonged to the Indians.

It is better to be honest and leave others' stock alone
Than to leave your native country and seek a Mexican home.

But Sam Bass hardly ran as far as the Mexican border to escape the angry redskins; after becoming separated from his companions and running about three hundred miles, he stopped at San Antonio.

If Sam could have run all his horses to San Antonio with him, here he could have played poker, faro, monte, or what he would, with the bottle passing around the table to celebrate each new deal, and he would have been happy.

But he had only his mount, the subdued race-horse; he sold that, bought himself an outfit, and hired out as a cowboy to Joel Collins, who wanted trail-hands to take a herd up to Deadwood.

The outfit

Sold out in Custer City and then went on a spree;
A harder set of cowboys you seldom ever see.

They drank it straight and swigged it mighty; and the six months' wages and all that Joel Collins had made on the sale lasted through the spree, but left not enough for a chaser to calm the next week's headache. Broke and in a far-away country, the outfit determined to rob the Deadwood coach. With Joel Collins and Sam Bass as the brains of the gang, the holdup was successful; it was followed by another and another, and the outfit lived hilariously and unmolested in Deadwood for some time. They left to stage a bigger and more artistic robbery; and on September 19, 1877, at Big Springs, Nebraska, they boarded the U. P. train, collected some five thousand dollars from the passengers, and made off with about one hundred and fifteen thousand dollars in twenty-dollar gold pieces from the express car. The gang would have shot the express messenger, but Sam Bass would not permit such coarse conduct.

The money was hidden, and the gang strolled about the streets of Ogallala while sheriffs and Wells-Fargo men and United States marshals hunted the country for some trace of the bandits.

When the excitement had died down, they

Split it up in couples and started out again. . . .
Sam made it back to Texas all right side up with care;
Rode into the town of Denton with all his friends to share.

It was seven years since Sam Bass had first come to Denton; now the proud citizenry boasted of him as a local boy. Sam made camp in Cave Hollow, and asked some of his old friends to call. Sam's proud record was common knowledge; his friends called, saw the gold, and six or seven joined under Sam to make their fortunes.

Sam's life was short in Texas; three robberies did he do,
He robbed all the passengers, mail and express cars too.

With Government marshals and hordes of public, private, and amateur detectives on the trail, Sam and his gang moved about Denton County, changing camp occasionally when a posse came too close; and when no posses came Sam made a public appearance and hurled defiance at law and order. Once a posse found the gang fast asleep, stole their horses and drove them to the Denton livery stable. But as they celebrated their exploit in an all-night dance hall, Sam Bass and his merry men came into Denton, stole back their horses, and silently rode away.

After the second train robbery to the credit of Sam Bass, the governor of Texas ordered Captain June Peak of the Texas rangers to Denton; the captain swore in seventy-eight young men and paraded into Denton, learned that Sam Bass was in camp four miles away, and discreetly went back to Austin.

The gang held up another train; and the governor ordered Captain Peak out again. This time the captain took with him several Texas rangers, old-timers, and went forth to do battle. One of Sam's men, called "Arkansas" for short, was killed, and two others were captured, one of them Jim Murphy.

Oh, what a scorching Jim will get
When Gabriel blows his horn.

For Sam Bass had befriended Jim; he had given him money and provisions when his wife and children were sick and Jim was broke; and the craven Jim Murphy betrayed Sam Bass to his death.

A few days after his arrest Murphy strolled into Sam's camp; he had jumped his bail, he explained, and was ready to take his old place in the gang.

In July, 1878, the gang rode out for another robbery. A note from Murphy to General Jones—"We are on our way to Round Rock to rob the bank. For God's sake, be there to prevent it"—gave the game away.

Sam Bass, Sebe Barnes, Frank Jackson, and Jim Murphy rode into Round Rock on the afternoon of the twentieth. Murphy fell back, to "stop and get some corn for the horses;" Sam and his companions tied their horses in an alley back of the bank, and sauntered into a store for tobacco. In the store were two deputy sheriffs; one approached Sam, and demanded his pistol. The shooting began; Sam shot the two deputies, but a crowd of citizens opened fire outside. The odds were too great. Barnes was killed at once, Sam Bass was wounded; and Jackson, shooting alone against thirty men, fought his way to the horses, helped his chief to mount, and rode away with him.

The next morning Texas rangers found Sam Bass alone, dying. He had ordered Jackson to leave him; and he died refusing to tell the names of those who had been in his gang.

Sam Bass had been a gallant swashbuckler; his defiance had been a grand gesture; he had been forced to shoot the only two men he ever killed. The miserable Jim Murphy was despised even by the rangers that had persuaded him to the betrayal, and in a few weeks committed suicide; the cow-country liked the boy from Indiana and kept alive his fame in the "Ballad of Sam Bass," and in the desultory narratives that were passed around with the tobacco.

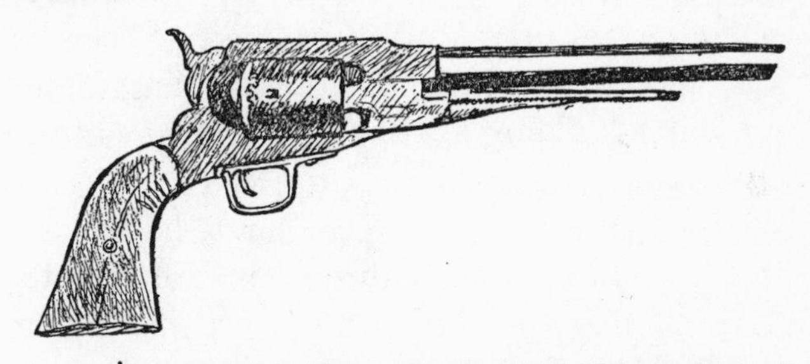

OLD CAP'N BALL SIXSHOOTER USED BY THE EARLY-DAY COWMAN

CHAPTER NINE

THIS MAN THE COWBOY

A SOUTHERN university plans to make a new hall a memorial to the cattle industry that brought the state its first prosperity; and if the bearded dons accede, on one of six plaques will be chiseled—not "In Commemoration of the Cowboy," not simply "The Cowboy," but—"Charlie Siringo, Cowboy."

And if we talk of Charlie Siringo rather than of the "typical cowboy," it is because the flesh-and-blood Siringo is more important than a myth.

He was born in 1855, in the "Dutch Settlement" of ten or twelve houses on a peninsula extending into the Gulf of Mexico. When he was old enough he got a little schooling, in an old frame building about a mile away from the settlement. Sometimes, to save his sunbrowned feet from the grassburrs, he walked on the Gulf sands; but then he was often late, from chasing the shadow of a sea gull flying along the beach, or galloping on his stick horse after sand crabs that for the moment were wiry-legged Longhorn steers running from his deadly lariat.

He "bummed around" for a time; and in the spring of 1871 he "hired out" to punch cattle for "Shanghai" Pierce, the owner of the Rancho Grande. At the ranch he was assigned to one of three outfits to round up cattle on the outlying range. "Being a store there we rigged up in good shape. I spent two or three months' wages for an outfit, spurs, etc., trying to make myself look like a thoroughbred Cowboy from Bitter Creek."

Three years later Siringo made his first trip up the Chisholm trail. "After a month's hard work we had the eleven hundred head of wild and woolly steers ready"—and the processional began.

The cattle were turned over to the trail-boss on a cold, rainy evening; and that night, in its baptism of rain and lightning, the herd stampeded. On the drive "everything went on smoothly with the exception of a stampede now and then," and with hard and skillful riding to manage an uneasy, half-wild herd, with long working-hours broken by occasional snatches of sleep, Siringo earned his sheepskin in trail-driving.

One day a wild, aimless shot of his, to scare off some dogs attacking a calf, hit his own dog. "No, no! I didn't feel bad; it was some other youngster about my size. I dismounted and caressed the poor dumb brute, with tears in my eyes. It was ten miles to camp or the nearest ranch, and therefore I had no alternative but to kill him—or leave him there to suffer and finally die. . . . I made several attempts to kill him, but every time I would raise the pistol to shoot he would look into my eyes so pitifully as much as to say please don't kill me. I at last mounted my horse and after starting off wheeled around and put a bullet between his eyes. Thus ended the life of as faithful a dog as ever lived."

After his first trail-drive, Charlie Siringo never deserted cowpunching, except for a few months' "vacation" now and then. He rode, worked, fought, drank; his home was his saddle, until——

"About the first of March I received orders from Mr. Beals, who was then at his home in Boston, Mass., to get everything in shape to start for the Panhandle at a moment's notice.

"That very night, after those orders were received, I fell head over heels in love with a pretty little fifteen-year-old, black-eyed miss, whom I accidently met. It was a genuine case of love at first sight. I wanted her, and wanted her badly, therefore went to work with a brave heart and my face lined with brass. It required lots of brass too, as I had to do considerable figuring with the old gent, she being his only daughter.

"Just three days after meeting we were engaged and at the end of the next three days we were made one. And three days later I was on my way to the Panhandle with an outfit of twenty-five men, one hundred horses and six wagons."

A vigorous life—and a sentimental life. . . .

Owen Wister traced the code of the cowboy back to Middle-English Chivalry; the cowboy was a knight-at-arms, the "Anglo-Saxon tradition" come to flower again. I have linked the cowboy with the Texas tradition, the code of personal dignity, personal liberty, personal honesty, of laconic speech and quick action, that was asserted in the Republic of Texas—a frontier that, by the very dangers it offered, attracted from the old states the blood of pioneers. We are both right, in our way; but Charlie Siringo would have laughed at us both, for trying to put in a phrase the way a cowboy carried his shoulders.

If Siringo is to be "explained"—if the cowboy is to be understood—the explanation lies in a paradox: a richly sentimental mind expressing itself in reticence, reserve, sententiousness, apparent indifference.

The reticence, the apparently unemotional exterior, was the product of his work and of the West in which he worked.

Said Major Shepherd, "The remoteness of other humans, and the charmed solitude of your temporary home, wraps you in selfishness; you are glad of your isolation. Everything around you is beautiful." The cowboy usually felt this beauty as contentment. "His point of view was that of the man on horseback;" he was an aristocrat. But in the solemn silence of the West his contentment was a quiet contentment; sure as he was of the inferiority of the rest of the world, except to his fellow-cowboys he seldom put that complacence into words.

The cowboy risked life and limb every time he mounted an unbroken horse; he never knew before he mounted whether his "outlaw" was the one vicious exception that could not be conquered. He faced a gamut of risks every time he worked in the branding pen, whether dragging cows to the fire or pressing on the iron; on every trail-drive, through stampedes, swollen rivers, lightning-storms. Cowpunching was man's work, and skilled cowboys were naturally proud and self-confident; but the danger was common danger, and because the cowboy traveled in "outfits," not alone, his satisfaction with his work was not to be spoken of. In the community of cowboys vanity could be expressed best by finery of clothes and equipment, not by words. The appearance of a gray-gloved, gray-Stetsoned cowboy in carefully combed chaps might be tacitly ignored by his fellows, or admired casually in some particular. The one response for such admiration was silence.

Best known of the cowboy's sentimentalities is his attitude toward women. His quiet gallantry has become a legend. In Dodge City (and it was a ticket to Dodge City that the railway-conductor in the story sold the drunken cowboy who boarded the train and demanded a ticket to hell), the courtesy of the cowboys and the residents toward women was proverbial; and some one unsteady on his feet who jostled a lady—a lady of whatever sort—would find himself knocked down by his nearest companion, as a warning against insulting a lady in Dodge City.

But this deep sentimentalism was sometimes blind; marriage acquired an uncomfortable sanctity, domesticity was the one end for women. As Charlie Post, cowboy, reasoned, "Why, the women had their husbands and children; what more has anybody thought necessary to woman's perfect happiness, than that she have her husband and children? They [the Westerners' wives] were happier than most; for added to love of husband and child was the knowledge of the necessity of their own existence and labors to the comfort and existence of those they loved."

As for the women who obviously weren't made for domesticity—there were times when the cowboy forgot his natural rôle of cavalier and respecter of women. There is record of several festive cowboys who hitched four unbroken bronchos to an old overland stage coach, filled the inside with ladies of the saloon, the revelers themselves clinging to the top or whatever part of the coach seemed to offer support, and let the coach go careening down the street while the banging of six-shooters and the screams of fair women offered accompaniment. But such tales are on record because of their rarity.

"I went to the bar and called for a toddy,

and as I was drinking it a girl came up and put her little hand under my chin, and looked me square in the face and said, 'Oh, you pretty Texas boy, give me a drink.' I asked her what she wanted and she said anything I took, so I called for two toddies. My, I was getting rich fast—a pretty girl and plenty of whiskey. I told the girl that she could make herself easy; that I was going to break the monte game, buy out the saloon, and keep her to run it for me when I went back to Texas for my other herd of cattle." Pleasantries of this sort—the toddies, the monte, the friendly gaze of the pretty little girl—may have been extravagant, but after the long succession of days on the dusty cattle-trail, when the one suggestion of woman was a photograph behind the tobacco-sack in the cowboy's shirt pocket, and there was only black coffee and tepid water to drink, the indulgence was a tonic.

Not even the cook carried whisky on the trail-drives, for every man had to work throughout the day and part of the night, and a drink-fuddled cowboy was dangerous as well as useless. And when the long drive was over the cowboys, weary of work and surfeited of coarse food badly cooked, naturally flocked to the pleasure-palaces of the cow-towns to celebrate. The Texas cowboys had known whisky-drinking as a social pleasantry on their home range; now they turned to whiskey in compliment to their new wealth; and from it some passed to the less polite indulgences, "the tinsel and tawdry glitter," that the cow-town impresarios had provided.

That the coming of the cowboys created the demand for vice was one of several flamboyant accusations of the righteous element in Kansas and Nebraska—the agrarian, non-stockowning element—when it began to discuss anti-trail legislation, and later when it began to discuss prohibition. About the time a Chicago financier was writing to the Bureau of Statistics of the Texas longhorns, ". . . intractable herds of half wild cattle, descendants of French and Spanish stocks of only common quality. They had to a degree degenerated by adapting themselves to natural conditions and surroundings of their habitation, Texas," Kansas editors were writing in similar deprecation of the Texas cowboys.

Very few cow-towns sprang up overnight to meet an anticipated demand. The meteoric career of one such Babylon, which when it was twenty-four hours old contained six saloons, a courthouse, and an "opera house," epitomizes

"COWBOYS IN TOWN!"

the history of these mushroom cities: after two days a cyclone demolished three saloons and the opera house; the following evening "desperados" on a spree almost wrecked the remaining saloons, and the canvas courthouse passed soon after, when a group of cowboys cut it up into overalls.

The "wild and woolly cow-towns"—Abilene, Ellsworth, and Hays City, on the Kansas Pacific Railroad, and Newton, Wichita, and Dodge City on the Santa Fe, and Ogalalla on the Union Pacific, these the most important—were born of the railroad. They came into existence one after another to flourish for a few years in a glamour that becomes more lurid as the "oldest inhabitants" compare the innocuousness of the Middle Western towns now with the times that were. Railroad men mingled with old buffalo-hunters; they demanded entertainment, and got it, before the first cattle-herds were driven up the trail.

The family, the pillar of society that rooted and stabilized the civilization that came with the passing of the range, was of little influence in shaping the society of the cow-country. Old home ties were broken almost imperceptibly, as a cowboy followed his calling for year after year. There were few of "the right kind of girls," and cowboys' wages did not permit much saving ahead against a start in domesticity. The cowboy who married was the exception. Without these two conventions—marriage and the family—nothing in the cowboy's society was more important than the cowboy himself. The individual reigned; self-poise, self-sufficiency, were normal. But with this lawlessness, this accepting of one standard only—his own—the cowboy was distinguished among men by his fidelity. All that his work required, all that his boss asked, he did—if his fellow-cowboys and his boss were friendly with him. A ranch outfit was a voluntary fraternity. Each man knew his own place, but felt that that place was as good as any other man's. If this fraternity failed, if the society on a ranch was shaken by petty jealousies and private quarrels, that outfit became known unfavorably on the range, and a cowboy who transferred from that ranch to another might have to wait months before his new fellows were ready to receive him as one of themselves.

The cowboy seldom complained to his fellow-cowboys, never to an outsider. Complaint was a petty vanity, either a wail that one had been given more than his share of work or the voicing of an irritation that all the cowboys in the outfit suffered in common, and needed no advertising. Cheerfulness must be maintained; or if not cheerfulness, silence.

Toward strangers this self-control became a strong reticence. It was this reticence that persuaded several "Pullman-car authors"—writers who learned the West from a car-window—that taciturnity was natural to the cowboy. To strangers, whether Easterners or Westerners, he was close-mouthed; but in his own group the cowboy could talk aimlessly, intimately, garrulously even. In the range yarns that he told he usually included detail that served only to make the stories longer.

But this intimate conversation, this small talk, was itself distinctive. Pithy, terse sentences were expected of the cowboy; in a lively group the conversation sometimes sparkled with a quick, slangy wit—like the conversation of the Old Cattleman in Alfred Henry Lewis' Wolfville stories.

This tendency to pithy speech had its violent expression; the cowboy swore for emphasis, for punctuation, by way of appreciation or condemnation. Sometimes a well-chosen word took the place of a sentence. Original combinations and a rich memory won for some Westerners a pleasant notoriety.

There was one Cassidy, cowboy turned outlaw, who was "hiding out" with his fellows at a little settlement on the Snake River, the only amusement drinking up the stock of the only bar in town, when Cassidy discovered an old widow, famous for her flock of chickens and even more for her profanity. He sought out the flock, and found the widow throwing grain to the poultry. Out came his gun; and he shot off the head of chicken after chicken. The widow's swearing as he shot was music to his ears; and when her repertoire was exhausted and she was retracing her way to its beginning, the delighted Cassidy sheathed his gun, threw down a twenty-dollar gold piece for each beheaded chicken, and rode away.

This terseness was a habit of thought as well as of speech. If a subject did not directly affect the cattle-country, the cowboy would not become interested. The geography of the West was common knowledge with every cowboy. This information he knew by his own travels—one trip up the Chisholm trail taught the insignificance of distance—and by the casual descriptions that other frontiersmen had given him. These things were concrete; they were about the West, and might some time be useful. But intangible, philosophical subjects were too vague, too impractical, to interest a man who thought incisively and quickly. Steve Hawes, "a cook with convictions," according to Philip Rollins, was moved to disgusted utterance: "Such things, they don't bring no facts to nobody. The feller that's a-goin' to do all the talkin', he just natcherally begins by pickin' out a startin' p'int that really ain't nowhars at all. He brands that startin' p'int 'Asoomin' that,' so he can know it if he runs acrost it agin. Then he cuts his thinkin' picket-rope, and drifts all over the hull mental prairie until he gits plumb tuckered out. And when he get so dog-gone tired that he can't think up no more idees to wave around and look purty in the wind, he just winds up with 'Wherefore, it follows.' Follows. Hell! It don't follow nothin'. It just comes in last."

Religion was among the philosophical subjects that gave the cowboy little concern. Healthy, hard-working, self-confident, as long as he followed the open range he was little troubled with speculation about hereafters. Charlie Siringo wrote of his mother's death, "With almost her last breath she begged me to make my peace with God, while the making was good. . . . I have been too busy to heed her last advice. Being a just God, I feel that he will overlook my neglect. If not, I will have to take my medicine, with Satan holding the spoon." And with most cowboys their speculations went no farther, except as they sang over the dreamy musings of some cowboy songs—such a one as:

Last night, as I lay on the prairie,
And looked at the stars in the sky,
I wondered if ever a cowboy
Would drift to that sweet by and by.
Roll on, roll on;
Roll on, little dogies, roll on, roll on. . . .

CHAPTER TEN

COWBOY SONGS

L. A. HUFFMAN, the photographer whose six thousand "Huffman Pictures" are a pictorial history of the West, wrote in praise of Charles Badger Clark: "Only yesterday I read aloud 'The Old Cow Man' to an old cow man, and when I had finished the stanza:

When my old soul hunts range and rest
Beyond the last divide,
Just plant me in some stretch of West
That's sunny, lone, and wide.
Let cattle rub my tombstone down
And coyotes mourn their kin,
Let hawses paw and tromp the moun'
But don't you fence it in,

he said in a choky voice and with more than a hint of moisture in his eyes, 'Who in h—— is this Clark anyway?' and he coughed up three bones for copies of the book."

And any one seeking the old pungency of

the cow-country will find in the poetry of Clark, of James Barton Adams, of Henry Herbert Knibbs, the jingle of the cowboy's spurs, "the swish of his rope, the creaking of his saddle gear, the thud of thousands of hoofs on the long, long trail winding from Texas to Montana," with the flavor in its fullness in the cowboy songs themselves. In these it is preserved better than many ex-cowboys can revive it now, their recollections tinctured by the boredom of these late years with a heavenly color.

The cowboy songs—easily available now in the collections of John A. Lomax and "Jack" Thorp—had no common origin. Some may have been brought from England and Scotland by younger sons who came to the New West for adventure and fortune; some were poems clipped from newspapers, and passed from camp to camp; some were parodies of old songs the cowboys remembered; some—the best—were composed by cowboys with a knack for robust, vivid phrases, and set to an old tune or to some sharp, unsophisticated rhythm that seemed naturally to belong to the words. Because these songs, whatever their origin, traveled from cowboy to cowboy mainly by oral rendition, the words were not always the same. Idioms crowded out conventional terms, the speech took on a colloquial ruggedness; and an English ballad, or some poem that a New York newspaper man had written, lived as a cowboy folk-song.

Sailors had hauled up anchors, split ropes, climbed halyards, to the rhythm of their own chanties, long before the day of the Western cowboy. And in the fo'c's'le they swapped yarns of the *Flying Dutchman,* of the fate of cap'n and crew on some ship that had taken a woman aboard, of the Old Man of the Sea and his tooth that ached for tobacco—and sometimes sang of ships and sailors' work:

Heave around the pump-bowls bright,
Leave her, Johnny, leave her.
There'll be no sleep for us to-night.
It's time for us to leave her.
Heave around or we shall drown.
Leave her, Johnny, leave her.
Don't you feel her settling down,
It's time for us to leave her.

The real kinship of the American cowboy is with the men on that everlasting frontier, the sea—a closer kinship than between the Western cowboy and the Argentine cowboy, or the Western cowboy and the Florida cowboys, gaunt, malaria-ridden men that Frederic Remington found shooting and stabbing each other "for the possession of scrawny creatures not fit for a pointer-dog to mess upon." Sailors might sing some chanty celebrating the ship's cook—

Our cook he is a very dirty man,
Sail away for the Rio Grande,
He cooks the food as dirty as he can.
Sail away for the Rio Grande,

and cowboys might sing together in celebration of their own camp cook—

You who linger long and listen to the things you like to hear
In the swell cafés in cities that to you are always dear
May think that I am partial to the cowboy and his grub
But I've dined at all those cafés and was fed once at a club,
And I've come to this conclusion, and right here I want to say,
When you eat at "Cafe Doughy's" you feel all right next day,
For here is Doughy's record, and beat it if you can—
He's cooked for us for twenty years and never lost a man.

Sailor or cowboy, each took on an unmistakable tang of his profession; with each his work was important enough to fill his "off hours" as well as his hours on duty.

The lumberjacks had songs whose even rhythm kept time to the fall of the ax; but after the day's work the stories of the lumberjacks were most likely not of the lumber-country as they knew it, but of a utopia that once was, in which Paul Bunyan, the Big Swede, and Hot Biscuit Slim did wonders. The Kentucky mountaineers had ballads praising the fighters and celebrating the bad men that once lived in them ther' hills; but they had no ballads describing the straining of the mash, no songs for the glory of the man with the hoe. The most remarkable thing about the cowboy songs is this obvious difference from the yarns and ballads of lumberjacks and Kentuckians: the cowboy songs deal with the cowboys' work.

Come, all you melancholy folks, wherever you
may be,
I'll sing to you about the cowboy whose life is
light and free;
He roams about the prairie, and at night when
he lies down,

CALF ROPING—NEVADA BUCKAROO

His heart is as gay as the flowers in May in his
bed upon the ground.

They're a little bit rough, I must confess, the
most of them at least;
But if you do not hunt a quarrel, you can live
with them in peace;
For if you do, you're sure to rue the day you
joined their band.
They will follow you up and shoot it out with
you, just man to man.

Did you ever go to a cowboy whenever hungry
and dry,
Asking for a dollar and have him you deny?
He'll just pull out his pocket-book and hand
you out a note,—
They are the fellows to help you whenever you
go broke.

Go to their ranches and stay awhile—they
never ask a cent;
And when they go to town their money is freely
spent.
They walk straight up and take a drink, paying
for every one,
And they never ask your pardon for anything
they've done.

When they go to their dances, some dance while
others pat;
They ride their bucking bronchos and wear
their broad-brimmed hats;
With their California saddles and their pants
stuck in their boots,
You can hear their spurs a-jingling and perhaps some of them shoots.

Come, all soft-hearted tenderfeet, if you want
to have some fun,
Go live among the cowboys, they'll show you
how it's done;
They'll treat you like a prince, my boys, about
them there's nothing mean;
But don't try to give them too much advice,
for all of them ain't green.

"The Old-Time Cowboy" is one of many such songs.

In a once-popular novel is written, "There was not an outfit which did not have its banjo player, its mandolin or its guitar, its harmonica and jews-harp performers, besides its dozens of stalwart fellows whose sweet but untrained voices were the joy of the camp." The idea of each group of cowboys as a sublimated barber-shop quartette is an old one; about it several vaudeville acts have been built, in which pink young men in blue silk shirts gather about a "campfire" with red paper streamers for flames, and render a few well-chosen ballads. But when the trail-herd had been bedded, or a day's work of rounding up cattle had been completed, the cowboys around the camp fire were more apt to smoke and talk, to "be reminded" of some incident of Indian-fighting down in Texas or something unusual that happened on a previous trail-drive, than to sing.

The cowboys sang as they rode night-guard on a herd, to keep themselves awake and to keep the cattle quieted. Will Barnes, cowboy, has suggested that the custom of singing to the bedded cattle was to drown out any unfamiliar noises that might make the cattle uneasy; but the soft, slow drawl of

When threatening clouds do gather and blind-
lightnings flash,
And heavy raindrops splatter and rolling
thunders crash,
What keeps the herd from running, stamped-
ing far and wide?
The cowboy's low, long whistle, and singing
by their side,

could not conceal the sharp howl of a coyote, or the crackling of a dry branch under the horse's hoof. The traditional explanation, that the cattle were kept at ease by the steady singing, and actually liked it, is better. Old Lake Porter always took his fiddle up the trail with him. "Often have I taken my old fiddle herd at night when on the trail, and while some of my companions would lead my horse around I agitated the cat guts. . . . And say, brothers, those old long-horned Texas steers actually enjoyed that music."

In the frontier towns and in the cow-towns, cowboys celebrated their holidays by going over the songs that all knew, then listening closely as one of their number, or some convivial stranger, sang them a ballad not so familiar. Warmed by a few glasses, some one might sing—

Come all you wild rovers
And listen to me,
While I retail to you
My sad history.
I'm a man of experience
Your favor to gain,
Oh, love has been the ruin
Of many a poor man.

When you are single
And living at your ease
You can roam this world over
And do as you please;
You can roam this world over
And go where you will
And shyly kiss a pretty girl
And be your own still.

But when you are married
And living with your wife,
You've lost all the joys
And comforts of life.
Your wife she will scold you,
Your children will cry,
And that will make papa
Look withered and dry.

Come close to the bar, boys,
We'll drink all around.
We'll drink to the pure,
If any be found;
We'll drink to the single,
For I wish them success;
Likewise to the married,
For I wish them no less.

And then the bartender would wipe his hands on his white apron, and set out the little glasses with the deceitfully thick bottoms; and the toasts would be drunk. Charles J. Finger and Joaquin Miller were in McClosky's saloon in San Angelo, listening to such an exchange of ballads and taking part themselves, when "a fellow with a predominant blue eye" commenced "The Texas Cowboy," but got only to the second verse—

Oh, I am a Texas cowboy
Far away from home;
If ever I get back to Texas
I never more will roam.

Montana is too cold for me,
The winters far too long;
Before the roundups do begin,
Our money is all gone.

"Things must have gone off at a tangent," continues Finger, "for Miller, a little in his cups, held that Montana was slandered. He held that the song was a libellous offense and the other regarded him dubiously for a moment, yet, withal, there was a touch of appreciation in his eye. Somehow I became involved, being called upon to decide between the relative merits of Texas and Montana, and I recall phases of my indecisions very distinctly. Then some one called for soda water, another opened a door and let in a draft of fresh air, and things were clear again."

Among the cowboy ballads that narrate the remarkable deeds of some men of the range country and the sad end of some who fell foul of the sheriff, are many that reveal a lively interest in the exploits of criminals and the derring-do of highway bandits. The fascination of the "lone riders" who lived for themselves alone, who delighted in the dangers of being pursued and risking gun-fire, stirred the imagination of cowboy poets. These ballads had their origin in cow-camps, and were shaped by the criticism of the cowboys themselves; and most of the zest and vigor would be lost if the verses should be polished and "civilized."

In the ballad on Jesse James that was known all over the cow-country—

Jesse went to rest with his hand on his breast;
The devil will be on his knee.
He was born one day in the county of Clay
And came of a solitary race—

the roughness is good because it is natural. "Jesse James" is more than a recital of the bandit's exploits; the ballad was born of the gusto, the joy in living, that expressed itself when a cattleman just made rich thundered to the chophouse waiter for a hundred dollars' worth of ham and eggs, and again when a cowboy forced his horse into a swirling flood to convince the steers on the point of the herd that the river was safe to cross.

Sam Bass, the train-robber, was celebrated in a ballad familiar the length of the range—

Sam Bass was born in Indiana, it was his native home,
And at the age of seventeen young Sam began to roam.
Sam first came out to Texas a cowboy for to be,—
A kinder-hearted feller you seldom ever see.

The ballad runs through his list of holdups, describes his four true companions and the false one that finally "framed" him; then—

Sam met his fate at Round Rock, July the twenty-first,
They pierced poor Sam with rifle balls and emptied out his purse.
Poor Sam he is a corpse and six feet under clay,
And Jackson's in the bushes trying to get away.

A song with some traces of a "literary" flavor disposes quickly and unsentimentally of Billy, the Kid. Billy was a callow, vicious youth, an out-and-out killer; the cow-country had no sympathy for his sort.

Billy was a bad man,
And carried a big gun,
He was always after greasers
And kept 'em on the run.

He shot one every morning,
For to make his morning meal.
And let a white man sass him,
He was shore to feel his steel.

He kept folks in hot water,
And he stole from many a stage;
And when he was full of liquor
He was always in a rage.

But one day he met a man
Who was a whole lot badder
And now he's dead,
And we ain't none the sadder.

Because facile rhymes and the good-fellow sentiment of the Edgar Guest-Berton Braley school of domesticated poetry are not the stuff of which cowboy songs are made, the cowboy song is peculiarly the cowboy's own. A recently started Western-story magazine began each of its first few issues with a "manufactured" cowboy song, but soon changed to reprinting each month a genuine cowboy ballad. There is room for only one "Out Where the West Begins," that ballad of Arthur Chapman's—

Out where the skies are a trifle bluer,
Out where friendship's a little truer,
That's where the West begins;
Out where a fresher breeze is blowing,
Where there's laughter in every streamlet flowing,
Where there's more of reaping and less of sowing,
That's where the West begins—

and that room is in the store-windows of village "art-shops," where its cloying verses, neatly engraved against a gold background and framed in imitation mahogany, may sit alongside Kipling's "If," and poems "To Mother" and "On Friendship."

"The Last Longhorn" is an epic in the vernacular:

An ancient long-horned bovine
Lay dying by the river;
There was lack of vegetation
And the cold winds made him shiver;
A cowboy sat beside him,
With sadness in his face,
To see his final passing,—
The last of a noble race.

The ancient eunuch struggled
And raised his aching head,
Saying, "I care not to linger
When all my friends are dead.
These Jerseys and these Holsteins,
They are no friends of mine;
They belong to the nobility
Who live across the brine. . . .

"I remember back in the Seventies,
Full many summers past,
There was grass and water plenty,
But it was too good to last.
I little dreamed what would happen
Some twenty summers since,
When the nester came with his wife, his kids,
His dogs, and his barbed-wire fence."

And the cowboy riz up sadly
And mounted his cayuse,
Saying, "The time has come when longhorns
And their cowboys are no use!"
And while gazing sadly backward
Upon the dead bovine,
His bronc stepped in a dog-hole
And fell and broke his spine. . . .

CHAPTER ELEVEN

ALKALI IKE IN BELLES-LETTRES

IN 1922 the hierarchies of literary criticism made official acknowledgment of the existence of the dime novel, when the exhibition room of the New York Public Library was turned over to a complete set of the Beadle and Adams paperback novels, catalogued not as "Curiosa Americana," but openly and defiantly as "Dime Novels." Now that the thin volumes which once were bought surreptitiously from dingy second-hand bookstores and smuggled into haylofts and attics have become the pride of librarians and the treasure of bibliophiles, it may be suggested that the dime novel cannot be dismissed as simply a literary curiosity. The exploits of Little Dan Deadshot, Young Wild West, Rattlesnake Ned, and their dashing companions have been widely read; and the dime novel has had its part in building the heroic galaxy of cowboy, gunman, buffalo-hunter and Indian-fighter that a public has cherished, and has affected the writing of Western stories by authors of more respectable mediocrity—contributors to the magazines and scenario-writers for the old photoplays.

The forerunners of the dime novel were the four-penny weeklies of New York, blatant publications, forever boasting of the immensity of their circulation and the unparalleled ingenuity and sensationalism of their writers. The greatest of these weeklies was the *New York Mercury,* for on its staff of serial writers was Edward Zane Carroll Judson, long worshiped as "Ned Buntline." Sea stories, border stories, tales of the Revolution—Ned Buntline could furnish them all, in quantity, and the grateful proprietors of the *Mercury,* by their own admission, paid him enormous sums. And when in 1857 Beadle started the publishing of dime novels, Ned Buntline had already developed the technique.

The greatest writers of dime novels have not been pale young men from Connecticut, but men who had known the frontier—"Bruin" Adams, Colonel Prentiss Ingraham, Colonel Cody ("Buffalo Bill"), Ned Buntline. The scope of the dime novel grew as the frontier grew; from looking backward, to "Sadie, a Heroine of the Rebellion," "Stella Delorme;

or, the Comanche's Dream," "The Black Avenger of the Spanish Main" (Tom Sawyer had read Ned Buntline!), the paperbacks turned to the West of their day, glorified the exploits of Buffalo Bill, Big Foot Wallace, Wild Bill, and used the background of these gun-toting warriors in fiction.

The West of the dime novels became a lurid background across which flamboyant caricatures stalked to shoot and be shot, because, before the West had been introduced into the dime novel, sensationalism had become a tradition not lightly to be broken, and because of the remarkable personalities of the more renowned authors.

The life story of Ned Buntline, the dean of the dime-novelists, is called by his biographer (no less a celebrity than "Wild Wildwood") "more thrilling than romance," but it is romance, mad romance. From before the mast as common sailor to midshipman, young Judson was snubbed by his fellows; he challenged thirteen of them in a day, fought seven, one after the other, marked four of his adversaries for life, did not receive a scratch, and made it known to the midshipmen and the world in general that he was as good as anybody. Beginning in these midshipman days, he wrote thrilling romances of the sea, novels read, we are assured, "by a host of warm admirers, who found the scene as realistic as any ever portrayed by Captain Marryat or Fenimore Cooper."

"Ned Buntline" (Judson had been eclipsed in his own literary splendor) was in the Seminole War, fought enthusiastically and with distinction, and heightened the contemporary literature by his account of how he killed a large jaguar in Florida.

Next he went up the Yellowstone as an agent of the Northwest Fur Company, and saw vast herds of bison, bands of elk, Rocky Mountain sheep, antelope—fertile literary material for one of the greatest swashbucklers American literature has known. Back again, "he wedded a lovely and intellectual young lady whom he met in the Sunny South, and stimulated anew to the exercise of his literary talent, he established a bright journal entitled *Ned Buntline's Own.*"

With the founding of the journal Buntline multiplied his output of thrillers, and he settled down, after a fashion, to the manufacturing of literature. He took a flyer in Americanism, and lent his pen and tongue to the Know-Nothing cause. The Civil War interrupted his flow of heroic sagas. Home on furlough, he overstayed his leave, and his lovely and intellectual young wife, to restore peace in the family, prevailed upon the sympathetic General Brown at Fort Hamilton to lock up the scribe. But in his few days of captivity, he wrote three bloodcurdling novels.

And in this hectic vein the life-story of this unplumed cavalier proceeds. At one time he, Buffalo Bill, Wild Bill Hickok, Texas Jack, Captain Jack Crawford, and a few others rambled over the Western plains, reveling in hunting and in Indian-fighting, leading an existence irresponsible and spectacular, while Buntline gorged himself with "local color" for thrillers in which all the *dramatis personæ* hunted and fought in the same careless, exaggerated fashion. Sensations upon sensations, riots, shootings, prisons, wars, emblazon the biography of this monstrous egomaniac, and sensations upon sensations emblazon his writings. The style was the man—florid, gusty, sentimental, belligerent. He made speeches on temperance, and in irrepressible egotism described delirium tremens as he had known it; he wrote of life on the Western border, and his public saw in the straight-shooting noble-souled frontiersman that his pages praised the hero of a hundred fights, Ned Buntline himself. With Ned Buntline as the dean of Western-border sensationalists, what chance had the cowboy of the dime novels to be more than half-way human?

His fellow-novelists followed the cue. So Colonel Cody's "Wild Bill, the Whirlwind of the West, or the Buckskin Braves of the Platte," begins with delectable tenderness, "Silently, beautifully, the snow floated down casting over the earth its downy covering," and proceeds to a gory carnival quite an improvement on the affairs of "Thanendanaga and Scourge" and "Red Ralph the Ranger" in the dime novels of the early seventies.

The greatest of dime-novel cowboys is Young Wild West, "the Well-Known Boy Hero and Champion Deadshot of the West." The "Wild West Weeklies," by "an Old Scout," are now in their twelfth hundred; through the dark days of war and against the growing urbanity of youth they have struggled on, though the price has risen from five cents to seven, and lately to eight, and the format has been reduced. In the issues of the last few years the adventures of Young Wild West and the companions who share his perpetual youth are followed by several pages of radio notes;

and with the burden of this humiliation, Wild West is becoming pallid and world-weary. Soon he, Young Jack Dashaway, Fullback Fred, the legion of messenger boys of Wall Street, and other heroes of the dime novel (Beadle's Dime Library has given this literature its name, whatever price it brings) will be without biographers, and the trade-name of "Old Scout" will be as legendary as "Bertha M. Clay."

Says "a tall, sinewy cowboy" to Young Wild West, "You sartinly do look peart. With that long hair of yours hangin' down over your shoulders an' a fancy buckskin coat an' trousers, you about come up to ther pictures we see sometimes. Then, ag'in, that red fringe on your clothes looks as though it might be real silk, and ther horse you're ridin' might be worth five hundred dollars." Of course his clothes were the most gorgeous, his horse the finest; for Young Wild West "who had made himself famous through his wonderful shooting and remarkable coolness," is the superman. His companions are Cheyenne Charlie, ex-Government scout, and Jim Dart, a Wyoming boy; Cheyenne Charlie's wife, Anna; Ariette Murdock, the sweetheart of the hero, and Eloise Gardner, Jim Dart's sweetheart. "The girls, as they always called them, had been riding about on horseback with our hero and his partner for something like two or three years now"—in each issue "two or three years," for in the *naïveté* of dime novels time has no place. The party is completed by two Chinamen, Wing Wah, the foil, "rather quiet, honest, and an excellent cook," and his Brother Hop Wah, the comedian of the party—"one of the most clever sleight-of-hand performers to be found anywhere, and being fond of practical joking, quick to think, he was certainly what might be termed an extraordinary Chinaman." With such characters as these, what worry is the narrative? Here is love interest, comic relief, adventure, a roving scene, and a perfect hero, who never misses a shot, never says an ungentle word, always succeeds whatever the odds, and offers his chivalrous service to all good causes and all fair ladies in distress. He finds Hoss Thomson, manager of Buckthorn Ranch, hard pressed by sheepmen driving a great herd across his range; he disperses the wicked sheepmen and saves the range from devastation, and goes on his way. He finds his old friend Lively Bick, ranchman, suffering from a gang of Apaches, "a whole lot smarter than what they look," rustling his cattle. Young Wild West shoots a few Indians, scares off the rest, and goes forth for further adventure. He attends a rodeo, outrides and outshoots a jealous cowboy, and foils that cowboy's attempt to steal a chest of gold. He finds a community harassed by "the Scourge of Red Rock Pass," a group of bandits called the Mystic Dozen, captures them almost single-handed—"There was lots of cheering then, and some of the excited men picked up the boy and carried him about on their shoulders."

Facile stuff, perhaps, naïve hero worship for bookkeepers and small boys. But if the hero-cowboy's virtue (the "Young Wild West" of these last years does not touch liquor!) was emphasized sometimes insufferably, and the cowboys suffered as a matter of weekly routine spectacular dangers that had practically passed with the buffalo-hunter and the Indian-fighter, there were other misconceptions—vicious misconceptions—in circulation at the heyday of the dime novel.

The cow-towns of the frontier had not resorted to Eastern subterfuges in concealing vice; and as tales of these American Sodoms came into the East, there came also tales of depraved creatures that made these towns possible. The account given its readers by the

Washington Star, January 1, 1878, is one of many: "Here (in the cow-towns) those nomads in regions remote from the restraints of moral, civic, social, and law enforcing life, the Texas cattle drovers, from the very tendencies of their situation the embodiment of waywardness and wantonness, and the journey with their herds, and here they loiter and dissipate, sometimes for months, and share the boughten dalliances of fallen women." Joseph Nimmo, Junior, prim and high-collared, had from his desk in the Bureau of Statistics office in Washington conducted an investigation of the economic condition of the cattle-country; but the limits of the information his correspondents had furnished him did not lessen the assurance of his article for *Harper's* on the American cowboy—"Upon slight provocation they would shoot down a fellow-man with almost as little compunction as they fired upon the wild beasts." One Mr. Thomas Holmes, enlightening the readers of the *Chautauqua Magazine,* was more lenient: "The cowboys of those times were men born and bred on the frontier and trained to the rough and unsentimental requirements of Indian warfare. Then they traversed the ranges armed to the teeth, alert to detect the presence of bloodthirsty savages at whom they would as soon send a bullet flying as to cast a lasso over the horns of a wild steer." He went on to explain that the present cowboy, while still uncouth, was more gentle.

The legend of the god-forsaken cowboy was endorsed in high circles. President Arthur, in his message of December 6, 1881, mentioned that in the West "a band of armed desperadoes known as 'Cowboys,' probably numbering fifty to one hundred men, have been engaged for months in committing acts of lawlessness and brutality which the local authorities have been unable to repress." On the third of May he issued a proclamation calling upon the cowboys "to disperse and retire peaceably to their respective abodes."

One regrets that dime novels had no part in the education of an Eastern politician. Their authors were at least entertaining; and their whole heroic philosophy hurled the lie at such widely read drivel as that article which thus disposed of the cowboys: "Four out of five, when sent to their last account, went through the medium of a deadly missile at the hands of an enraged or drunken companion or by the obnoxious noose of an outraged community or vigilance committee."

In the dime novels, if not in the American monthly magazines, the cowboy was nature's nobleman: "He was a man not over twenty-four," writes "Harry Hawkeye" of "Calvin Yancey, the colonel's trusted chief," "straight as an arrow, fair and ruddy as a Viking, with long, flowing golden hair, which rippled over his massive shoulders, falling nearly to his waist; a high, broad forehead beneath which sparkled a pair of violet blue eyes, tender and soulful in repose, but firm and determined under excitement. His entire face was a study for a sculptor with its delicate aquiline nose, straight in outline as though chiselled from Parian marble, and its generous manly mouth, with full crimson and arched lips, surmounted by a long, silken blonde mustache, through which a beautiful set of even white teeth gleamed like rows of lustrous pearls." It remained for Owen Wister to raise this cowboy-superman from *sub rosa* literature to respectability and recognition. Though Wister probably never knew it, the Virginian was a true kinsman of Calvin Yancey, the young cowboy chief.

CHAPTER TWELVE

THE VIRGINIAN AND TAISIE

IN 1885 a thin-chested young Bachelor of Laws from Harvard set out for the West to regain his health. "Wyoming burst upon the tenderfoot resplendent, like all the story-books, like Cooper and Parkman come true again; here, actually going on, was that something which the boy runs away from school to find, that land safe and far from Wednesday morning, nine o'clock and the spelling-book; here was Saturday eternal, where you slept out-of-doors, hunted big animals, rode a horse, roped steers, and wore deadly weapons." And Owen Wister, "escaped from civilization's schoolroom," entered with a whole-souled vigor into this new democracy. When his health was regained, he returned to Philadelphia, and entered the bar; but the ranch in Wyoming ultimately had a stronger appeal than the court rooms of Philadelphia. Wister made several visits to the West, affected a careless loose-tied bow in place of the traditional black ribbon of his profession, had photographs taken of himself in shirt-sleeves—and began to write Western stories.

Twenty years later Wister thought of those days when he began his first tale of the West, and he became sentimentally loquacious. "Living men, not very old yet, have seen the Indian on the war-path, the buffalo stopping the train, the cowboy driving his cattle, the herder watching his sheep, the government irrigation dam, and the automobile—have seen every one of these slides, which progress puts for a moment into its magic-lantern and removes to replace with a new one," he wrote. "The nomadic, bachelor west is over, the housed, married west is established."

But the nomadic, bachelor West had not been forgotten in the hasty, subduing Easternization the years had brought; there was the painting of Frederic Remington, there was the life of Theodore Roosevelt, there was the literature of Owen Wister.

When Wister wrote those episodes later gathered into the volumes *The Virginian* and *Lin McLean,* he wrote with the fervor of a missionary. It was his part to bring the real West into American *belles-lettres*—in his own words, to "disperse the Alkali Ikes."

The modest talent of Mary Hallock Foote had been used to present the sage-brush country sympathetically and intelligently; but hardly any one read her stories, and no one imitated her. Bret Harte had been read carelessly, and his humorous exaggerations had contributed to an Eastern ideal of Western America, in which red-shirted miners, pistol-carrying cowboys, dare-devil stage-drivers, flashy gamblers, and strange and lurid women live in a world Morley Roberts has called "a kind of kaleidoscopic harlequinade, ending up in a snow storm or the smoke of a gun-powder massacre."

Wister evidently thought himself well fitted for his task. In 1884 William Dean Howells had felt his literary pulse and found it promising (Wister's own metaphor), "a quickening came from the pages of Stevenson; a far stronger shove next from the genius of *Plain Tales From the Hills;* during an unusually long and broad wandering . . . the final push happened to be given by Prosper Mérimée." From Henry James came a later impetus: "In 1896 I sat with him and he went over my first book, minutely pointing out many things. Everything that he said I could repeat this moment, and his own pages have continued to give me hints without end." Wister's first tale was written with that self-sacrifice which is the author's duty to his work: "I left some good company at a club dinner table one night to go off to a lonely library and begin it."

The Virginian appeared as a novel in April, 1902. It was received enthusiastically; before the end of the year it had been reprinted fifteen times. In the next few years reprinting followed reprinting; there appeared also a "special edition in paper covers," a "theatrical edition," a "new illustrated edition," and in October, 1911, a "special limited edition." Now *The Virginian* sells more slowly, outclassed by many of its fellows in the "more than 500 titles of the best recent copyright fiction in popular priced editions."

At its first appearance the publishers evidently classified it as summer fiction and nothing more—but reviewers at once acclaimed it as a popular classic. One of the first said that Wister had "blazed the way to that quite possible impossibility, the American novel." H. W. Boynton, in the *Atlantic Monthly*, sang the Virginian as "a figure of splendor," of "superb aboriginal simplicity," and became naïvely exultant over the heroine, "the great triumphs of her love, first over social, and second over moral fastidiousness." Only a few reviewers, writing in hopelessly intellectual periodicals, seemed to realize that this romantic novel was not also an epic novel. Wrote Frank Jewett Mather, "When that perversity which prompts one to challenge any frank and spontaneous enjoyment wreaks itself on the *Virginian,* it finds surprisingly little to take back from the first enthusiasm." Most readers added to the first enthusiasm a second—the book was so fetchingly American. As Wister characteristically stated, in 1911, "If this novel is anything more than an American story, it is an expression of American faith."

If Wister had done what he set out to do, the history of the Western scene in American literature would have been changed greatly for the better.

Wrote Wister of *The Virginian,* "Any novel which presents faithfully a day and a generation is of necessity historical; and this one presents Wyoming between 1874 and 1890." Again he had valued his own work too generously. *The Virginian* does present, in a pleasant and readable fashion—the Virginian. "Lounging there against the wall was a slim young giant, more beautiful than pictures. His broad, soft hat was pushed back; a loose-knotted, dull-scarlet handkerchief sagged from his throat; and one casual thumb was hooked in the cartridge-belt that slanted across his hips. He had plainly come many miles from somewhere across the vast horizon, as the dust upon him showed. . . . The weather-beaten bloom of his face shone through it duskily, as the ripe peaches look upon their trees in a dry season. But no dinginess of travel or shabbiness of attire could tarnish the splendor that radiated from his youth and strength." Such was the Virginian—Young Wild West groomed, his *naïveté* replaced by the quiet wisdom that comes with power, less of a crusader, but still a man among men. If *The Virginian* were "our last glimpse of the pioneer in the plainsman and cowboy types, then passing and now gone," as a critic has called it, then our last glimpse was of a cowboy hardly a type at all; for Wister has labored to make the Virginian distinctive, one actually revered by his fellow cowboys. Lin McLean, young, soft-hearted, much given to rough banter and practical jokes, "one of the boys," is much more a type, much more a cowboy, than the irresistible Virginian ("As we drove by the eating-house, the shade of a side window was raised, and the landlady looked her last upon the Virginian. Her lips were faintly parted, and no woman's eyes ever said more plainly, 'I am one of your possessions.' ").

"A cowboy without cattle," writes Andy Adams, "is comparable to a lord without lands or a master without slaves." It is strange that Wister could have called his *Virginian* a historical novel of the cattle-country when there is not one scene set on the range among the cattle, when the cowboys seem throughout to spend their days in playful pranks, in love-making, in thief-hunting, in anything except work. Perhaps Wister believed that he had caught the spirit of the cattle-country, in the character of his hero and in the humorous by-play that enlivens the book, and could have gained nothing by introducing elements of life on the range at the expense of the love-interest. The great love of the Virginian for Molly Wood, the school-teacher from Vermont, is the unifying thread that binds the succession of incidents into a novel; and this great love is no more Western, no more related to "American faith," than the great loves of the fine young men in the drawing-room tales and desert-island romances of Louis Tracy, Morgan Robertson, and the Reverend Cyrus T. Brady.

Wister interrupts his narrative, in the approved fashion of the romancers of his day, to speculate on the mysterious thing called love, the grand passion so essential to his craft: "Has any botanist set down what the seed of love is? Has it anywhere been set down in how many ways this seed may be sown? In what various vessels of gossamer it can float across wide spaces? Or upon what different soils it can fall, and live unknown, and bide its time for blooming?" And this is the essence of *The Virginian:* the tale of one seed in its particular vessel of gossamer alighting in a spot of the West, of the sprouting of that seed, of the hazards of its growth, of its maturity. It could as well have landed somewhere else than in the Northwestern cattle-country; *The Virginian* would still have been *The Virginian.*

"Editors have at times lamented to me that good work isn't distinguished from bad by our multifarious millions," wrote Wister. "I have the happiness to know the editors to be wrong. Let the subject of a piece of fiction contain a simple, broad subject and the better its art, the neater its success; although the noble army of readers will not suspect that their pleasure is largely due to the skill." The dexterity with which Wister himself manufactured a "best seller" is not to his credit as an artist; for in his stressing of the "simple, broad appeal," the cattle-country that he loved and wanted to make live in literature has become the stuff of incident, a restraining grace that gives *The Virginian* color but is not permitted to mold its life.

It was not until nineteen years after *The Virginian* that another honest attempt was made by a literary craftsman to give the West of the cowboys an honorable place in American fiction. Emerson Hough knew the West from his own experience; and at the beginning of his career, before his success as a novelist had made him something of a dilettante in the American scene, writing novel after novel of places beyond the limited experience of most fiction-writers, he had written *The Story of the Cowboy.* This was in 1895; and Hough knew then that the day of the cowboy was passing. "Before many years have passed . . . we shall listen in vain for the jingle of his spurs, or the creak of his leather gear, or the whipping of his scarf end on the wind. Tinkle and creak even now die away in the distance beyond." With a wisdom beyond Wister's, Hough knew that the cowboy and the range were inseparable. "If we study him, we shall study also the day in which he lived, more especially that early day which saw the opening and the climax of that drama of commerce—the cattle industry of the West."

In 1923, when *North of 36* was written, Hough had been long enough a contributor to the *Saturday Evening Post* to know that fiction, to be successful in every sense as a serial and as a novel, had to have not only conflict, the essence of all fiction, but love. Life, as well as fiction, Hough saw as a succession of conflicts. In his own words, "It seems that there is implanted in nature and in the universe the law of two opposing forces; centrifugal and centripetal; good and evil; . . . that which sows to reap, and that which reaps where it has not sown." The story of a great conflict was inseparable from the story of the West, where men fought with men, and men fought with nature. But love—love in the cow-country was a brusque thing, an incident and not the aim of life in this woman-starved country with its iron traditions of clanship between men. Yet in the novel love must be the final reward; so with the first trailherd from Texas to Kansas in 1867—the drive that is the splendid theme of *North of 36*—there came a woman.

"The boss of Laguna del Sol stood framed in the doorway, in man's garb of shirt and trousers—an assumption shocking in that land and day. Obviously, now, she was tall, slender, supple, rounded to a full physical inheritance of womanly charm. . . . Against the morning light the freckles of Anastasie Lockhart could not be seen. No matter. Every man of these could have told you the number and contour of them all. In a way, too, they could have told you that her freckles went with her hair." The novel owes much to Hough's selection of Taisie Lockhart, herself a part of the cattle-country, as his heroine—rather than a commonplace little prude from Vermont that only Mary Wilkins Freeman could have made likeable. McMasters, the Virginian of the story, is worthy of her; he dominates, but he never struts. He too could have lived only on the Western range.

"'Light, stranger!' Nabours gave the arrival the usual greeting of the land. A dozen pairs of eyes gave him appraisal of the range. But the etiquette of the range was custom with this visitor. Though he was forced to wheel his horse quite about to do so, he dismounted on the same side of his horse as that which his hosts held, and not upon the opposite, or hostile, side. Moreover, he unbuckled his revolver belt and hung it over the horn of his saddle before entering the door. So! He had good manners. He was welcome."

The novel begins in poverty-stricken Texas, with word brought by McMasters of a waiting cattle-market to the north. The drive to reach Abilene is the story of *North of 36*.

"'Ef we don't make Aberlene it's because there ain't no Aberlene. Here we come, forty-five hundred cows, ef you don't mind calling 'em that, sixteen more or less human cow hands, nineteen kinds of rifles and six-shooters, a hundred and fifteen saddle ponies and the only red-headest boss in Texas, which is a girl. God bless our home!'"

With the villainy of a group of carpetbagger ruffians to fight, and danger after danger of the cattle-drive to overcome, proceeds the most faithful story of the cattle-country ever written by one not a cowboy himself. Hough has been far more diligent in his fidelity than he need have if his aim had been only to write a successful novel.

Hough had been in the Southwest first in 1881; he had lived and traveled in the West all his life. But this was not enough. From "the classic of the cattle trade," the rare *Historic Sketches of the Cattle Trade of the South and Southwest,* by Joseph G. McCoy, Hough has taken fact and atmosphere. As McCoyne, "the mayor of Abilene," Hough introduced McCoy himself into the narrative. "'I declare, I don't believe there is a coffin in this whole town—our storekeepers is that negligent, got that poor notion of goods,'" the mayor admits. "'Now think of my getting so busy, forgetting to have our merchants order plenty of coffins! I don't want Abilene to be back of no town in Kansas. You understand, in the hurry of getting things started gentlemen, a man's liable to overlook a lot of things.'"

Hough knew the novels of Andy Adams, the biography of Charlie Siringo, *A Lone Star Cowboy;* and the first volume of brief stories of trail-drivers about themselves, *The Trail Drivers of Texas.* The description of a terrific lightning-storm, the stories told in the hazing of a tenderfoot in the outfit, and the incident of that astonishing creature, no larger than a calf, bearing a spread of horns that would have been the pride of any venerable Longhorn steer—horns that came off once a gullible cattle-buyer had wagered that the creature could not possibly be a yearling—have been taken almost word for word from the volume of the trail-drivers.

Perhaps, if Hough had written *North of 36*

before he became an established novelist, the novel might have been as splendid as the theme. But with the florid carelessness that often comes with the need of filling many columns, Hough can be exasperatingly Zane-Greyish. He speaks of Taisie's father, "Colonel Burleson Lockhart, these two years deceased—a strong man in his day, and a poignant"; he says of Taisie, "She rose and went to the door, framed once more against the sun; and sixteen pairs of eyes of silent men went with her." When a crux arises in Taisie's love-affair, she lapses into a pseudo-Victorian jargon—this, for instance: " 'Sir, this is not easy to listen to!' She sank back on her rude fireside seat, trembling. 'I wish you had not come! I wish I had never seen you!' " Taisie's ethical code is almost that of a Middle-Western housewife, with only sparks of the freedom of the range-days of Texas. This ethical defect is Hough's. He cannot describe the night-life of Abilene without squirming. "The fumes of liquor, the reek of packed humanity, filled each insignificant room along Liquor Lane in Abilene. Especially crowded were the two more ambitious places, where dancing was obtainable in connection with strong drink. Here the scene was such as might best be forgotten as a part of the record of the outlands. There were a dozen or more women, or those who had once been women; and with these, in an obscenity that should balk any one, a hundred or two hundred men danced."

But—"Don't forget Jim Nabours and old Alamo," said an ex-cowboy as we talked over *North of 36*. "They are the gen-u-wine stuff—and they make the book." And he puffed a great cloud of tobacco-smoke to clinch his praise.

The old-timer meant that Hough had not allowed his cowboys to become types, but had made each man in the outfit as distinct, as self-sufficient, as he really must have been. Jim Nabours, the old foreman; Sanchez, old and gray, with his fighting-cock perched on the pommel of his saddle; Cinquo Centavos, the "boy" of the outfit; even old Alamo, the lead-steer—each is a picture to himself. "I'll bet that old dun coaster that's done elected himself head leader has got horns six feet acrost, an ef he's ten year old he's a hundred. Well, anyhow, he's on his way north. *And-a-lay,* old Alamo!' " Each cowboy in this "wild, unprepossessing band" has been created out of a fellowship that is a finer tribute to Hough than any woman could have paid him. "Bearded,

EARLY TEXAS TRAIL BOSS

hard, rude, unbrushed, they made a wild group when they stumped up to the morning fire, where each squatted on one knee while using tin cup and tin plate. Cutlery was scanty, but each man had some sort of knife. Sugar there was none, but a heavy black molasses did for sweetening the coffee, which itself was made largely of parched grain. A vessel of great red beans had been hidden in the hot ashes overnight; there was plenty of bacon aswim in the pans for spearing; and of corn pones, baked before the fire, many lay about." Hough knew and understood the cowboy; and his enthusiasm for his theme is pervasive and irresistible.

Of the cattle-trail, uniting North and South, he writes, "Here was the first break—the penetration of a peaceful, natural commerce here on the Western plains. Through that opening, in the years immediately to come, flowed values greater than those of barter and trade in horned kine. A manly understanding passed back and forth, and out of that tacit union, a concord in all young strong impulses. That union of North and South built the West overnight. The world has never seen a better country. That empire gave us our first and only true American tradition—the tradition of the West." It is about the making of that tradition, and the cowboy's part, that *North of 36* is written. *North of 36* is not a great book, because Hough was not a great novelist; but as a mirror of its chosen day it is faithful and reverent.

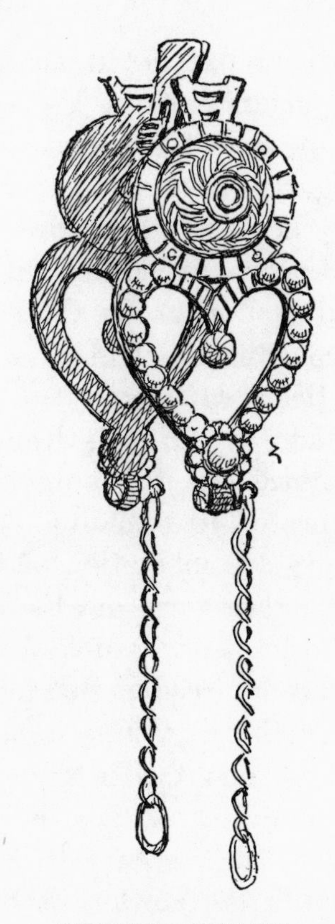

CALIFORNIA SPADE BIT

CHAPTER THIRTEEN

THE COWBOY PIGEONHOLED

THERE is no parallel in our literature for the importance of the Western scene in the popular fiction of the day. Some magazines, their garish covers shouting their presence on every news-stand, are devoted to it exclusively. Lately publishers have cleverly linked the attraction of the West with some other popular fancies. Out of such a union came *True Western Stories* and the curious *Ranch Romances.* "Ranch Romances," the editors announce, "is the only magazine in America dedicated to romantic Western life. Our stories are a combination of the ever-entertaining Western yarn and the age-old love story. Through the pages of *Ranch Romances* we aim to lead our readers out into the great open spaces and carry them away from the complexities of civilization into a world of simple feeling and direct emotion." For the West is more than a scene—it is a motif, as love is a motif; the cowboy is more than a character—he is an ideal.

By the editorial statements themselves, the aim of this cowboy literature is to transport the reader, whether high-school girl or twentieth-century cowboy, from the routine of things as they are to a semi-historical, primitive utopia. Entertainment is the all-in-all; and if occasionally some one of fair intelligence writes to suggest that popular literature may be something more than a formulated diversion for formula-ridden readers, the editor feeds pap to his own sense of inferiority by writing in his personality-columns (all the western-story magazines have these informal, "heart-to-heart" sections) of his correspondent as a scurvy creature, and continues to quote a reader from Peoria, "I surely love to read *Cowboy Stories,* because it is right there!"—one from Hawaii who writes "*Cowboy Stories* cannot be equaled by those in any other magazine—they are too superior"—and one from Chester, Pennsylvania, "You folks are getting out a corking magazine. You editors know how to pick stuff." An instance of this sort of reproof that deserves to become classic appeared recently: "Often some high-brow critic pauses long enough in his efforts to uplift American literature to sneer, with smug self-complacence, at stories of western romance," wrote the erudite editor. "As a rule he finds them superficial, 'illiterate,' written by amusement purveyors, who violate all the classic rules of story-telling." He proceeds to refute his high-brow critic by citing a high-brow, "himself a well-known writer and literary authority," the "himself" the English lady whom playgoers remember pleasantly for her "Will Shakespeare" and "A Bill of Divorcement"—Clemence Dane.

By reading the short stories in one of these cowboy story magazines—one picked at random will do—we may find how the cowboy has changed from the strong, simple, man of action that he was when Colonel Prentiss Ingraham and the Old Scout left him.

The issue before us begins with a complete novel, *The End of the Trail,* of which the editor explains, "Coming into the West was the Great Adventure for Nan Coburn. . . . Nan opened to Love in the form of a wind and sunburned man of the plains and found happiness in his arms." There is a temptation to linger here, with an old friend; for if the wind and sunburned man is not as distinguished as Young Wild West, surely he is as noble.

Putting a Crimp in Romeo has to do with "a tall, slim kid, white-skinned and plomb onsophisticated in the ways o' the cow-country, who's come out to Arizona a-chasin' health." The kid gets work at a ranch, and furnishes much sport for the cowboys; "then, for the Christmas holidays, Maizie McGriffin comes home from the school she's attending over in San Antone." Love comes to both (of course), but the old cattleman, the ranch-owner, decides to pit his strategy against the couple. The kid is given six months to earn ten thousand dollars, if he is to get the old man's consent; and by staking out a homestead claim on a water-site near the ranch, he gets the ten thousand from the old cattleman himself, in return for the water-rights. "It was to Youth this wise old rancher took off his hat and put up his gun," comments the enthusiastic editor.

Two Silver Spurs is a tale of the coming of the boss's cousin for a visit to the ranch, and the fight of a cowboy to win her love. She thinks him brutal, and refuses to go to a circus with him. The cowboy is shot by a convenient villain; and when the villain returns to complete his work, the girl saves the wounded suitor; and in return he rescues her when the same villain becomes insulting.

In *Harmony at Flood Tide* an itinerant preacher makes his camp near a ranch, and his daughter becomes fond of one of the cowboys. "And so romance came to dwell on the windswept prairies for a time and a new light glowed in the eyes of Mary Ellen. . . . And only the wood-doves knew that for two love-starved mortals, the gates of heaven had opened." Her father, caught in a flood, is lassoed and made to perform the marriage ceremony or else be jerked into the waters.

In *The Dewlapped Sleeper,* Blondy, a roving cowboy, wanders up to a ranch-house and rescues a girl and her mother from fell villainy. The girl interests him; "His inherent spirit of protectiveness was aroused, he wanted to champion her cause, but unschooled as he was in the ways of women he could not define the unspoken appeal of her." Her late uncle has concealed in something beginning with "d" half of the coin on which he scratched his will; the cowboy decides that the something is the dewlap of a pet steer, and so it is. The villain returns; but the pet steer suddenly becomes vicious, and attacks him. "It was all over in a matter of seconds. Blondy went and stooped over the silent thing that once had been a man."

The Rustler tells of a cattle-thief for whom a young lady conceives a sudden affection; she gives him a job on her father's ranch, and marries him.

We put the magazine aside. . . . Young Wild West was never like this. We take up another magazine; and again we find rustlers reforming because of a great love, cowboys winning their maidens in extraordinarily clever fashion, rapacious villains, ranchmen's daughter's, beautiful school-teachers, ranchmen's nieces, sheriff's daughters, in a profusion that makes us wonder if this West were not a Moslem's paradise. . . .

The secret of these Western short-stories is that they are not Western at all. As the rubber-stamp formulæ recur and recur—the appeal of woman in distress, villainy for villainy's sake, the legend of woman as a clinging vine, the triumph of wits over power and brawn, the surprise-finish technique, the confusion of mixed identities, the nobility of misunderstood men who shield weakling brothers and ladies' honor, the pathos of lost love—it becomes evident that very few of the situations depend on the West for such vitality as they have. These are formulæ common to all the popular-fiction magazines that do not attract "names;" and the West is dragged in, sometimes with shameful violence, as a fifth-rate stock company uses one tattered back-drop for act after act. The appeal of the Western background is assured; the movies attend to that. A West with love-at-first-sight is offered us, when the least we want is a West with heroics. And how much of the popularity of this short-story West is its popularity with writers who see in a coarse setting an excuse for coarse writing?

In most of those stories that could be laid only in the cattle-country, humor dominates in dialogue and situation.

In the spring of 1923 the *Western Story Magazine* presented a short story by Emerson Hough, "Curly's Coon." Its refreshing humor is more and more appreciated as the mechanically boisterous tales of a Ray Humphreys and Ray Nafziger, the most praised of the Western-story humorists, continue to appear.

" 'Cow hands gits thirsty, and look at them!' Curly argues. 'Now you take a man from back East that will only drink out of a bottle with four colors in the lay-bill—he's marked for a early tally in the new angel class. Not so with them like you and me, Sir Algernon, who know that everything is all right ef you want it an' kin git it. All the animiles know that.' " But Sir Algernon remonstrates: " 'Curly, your story doesn't hang together. Animals know what's good for them, and they never give way to intemperance, like cow-punchers and other depraved classes.' 'What else kin they git to drink?' demanded Curly. 'S'pose you was deprived of the power o' speech, as well as the price o' drinks, an' was dressed up in a hide worth anywhere from six bits to fifty dollars, an' had feet to run away with—would you be saunterin' down to the Lone Star fer a drink, or would you be pullin' fer the tall woods? An' what is they to drink in the tall woods but water? Look at us right now, an' you git the answer to that. Only reason animiles don't drink coffee or something else is that they can't git it. Now, I can prove that.' " And so is launched the story of Ebenezer, the coon that strayed into the cattle-country and became the pet of ol' man Wright's cow camp.

" 'He liked coffee, an' he et everything, without no regard to diet whatever.' " Curley and Ebenezer struck up a firm friendship. " 'I got right fond o' Ebenezer—he was so faithful to me, an' so useful. He could play as good a hand o' poker as any one o' the boys. He'd set on my shoulder an' look at my hand when I'd made my draw, an' if I happened to need an extra king or ace—why, Ebenezer'd go an' git it without no training at all. He'd hand me a card with one hand while he was attractin' the attention o' the next feller by puttin' his foot down the back of his neck. His front feet was always right cold, so this was hard to git used to, although it was one o' his favor-ite amusements.' "

There came to the ranch ol' man Wright, his charming daughter, and the Reverend Mrs. Reginald Jones-Valentine, " 'one o' them permanent ladies that goes in fer suffrage an' temperance an' everything else that men don't like.' " About dinner-time Miss Evie mixes " 'a dishpanful o' something that smelled so much like peace an' joy that even Ebenezer quits fluffin' about bein' asleep.' "

The sight of the dishpanful arouses the permanent lady. " 'Sir!' says Mrs. Reginald, pointin' with one finger down into the dishpan. 'This is a insult!' " In her ire she makes a fatal analogy: she points to the brute Ebenezer. " 'You have not even the intelligence o' that poor dumb brute,' says she. 'Men—vile men—are the only creatures knowed in nature which will put a enemy into their mouth fer to steal away their brains.' " But Ebenezer approached the punch pan. "He looked over it, then he turns an' gazes up at me, winks one eye, and breaks into the happiest smile ever seen on anybody's face. I knowed that he come from Arkansaw."

And the cowboys are almost as delightful as the coon. The idiom is delightfully exaggerated, but it is not made a dialect. The cowboys are an inordinately clever outfit; but they are cowboys.

Turning to Ray Humphreys, we find tales of a horse-race in which the villains plot to spill glue on the hero's saddle, of a rodeo with its coterie of amusing villains who plan to make a horse buck by pouring carbolic acid under the saddle. But delectable as all this is, the greatest of the humorists now writing for the Western-story magazines is Ray Nafziger. "Mr. Nafziger," writes his editor, "succeeds logically to the place of America's greatest humorist. He has been justly called 'the new Mark Twain with a touch of O. Henry.' Nowhere else can be found so shrewd a student of human nature and at the same time so brilliant a writer. It is with just pride that we announce Mr. Nafziger as one of the greatest humorists of the day!" One paragraph will do: "And then there was the kind-hearted cowboy I oncet knew what found a li'l orphan baby skunk and named her Emmaline, and that li'l skunk she would follow that cowboy around everywhere he went. So that cowboy he went callin' on his best gal and Emmaline she got jealous like all feemales do and perceeded t' bust up that courtship then and there."

This, then, is the cowboy as he usually is presented in the Western-story magazines: a woman-chaser or a mountebank.

The historical fidelity of these cowboy-stories is not always a matter of much concern. Writers for the *Frontier,* easily the best of the Western-story magazines, are generally accurate. For those writers that seek the tang of the cow-country as a matter of professional pride, the degree of faithfulness varies widely. But there must be some care; writers for *Adventure* and *Western Stories* cannot hope to create "realism" simply by the use of a little slang and a few Spanish words. For there are subscribers akin to those movie-goers who sit through a second showing to verify their list of flaws, and "old-timers" with a scent for fraud who are quick to write irate letters to the editor.

Frank C. Robertson is conspicuous among his fellow-contributors by a careful and intelligent use of the Western scene, by the quiet ease of his characters, who seem Westerners in their own country. With a straightforward, undistinguished style, and with plots always grounded in some conflict of villainy and virtue, he succeeds largely by his reticence. His people do not rant; like good Westerners, they have no time for playing to the gallery. And Robertson does not intrude a running fire of comment, with disquisitions on the sexual evolution of the heroine and on the hereditary might of the hero—a practice with much to recommend it commercially. One paragraph from *The Valley of Desolation* will suggest Robertson's effective use of trite situations by treating them simply and unsentimentally:

"She could feel his lips brushing her hair. She started to struggle, but common prudence restrained her. They were sitting on the very edge of a forty foot abyss, and at the bottom were sharp, projecting rocks like bayonets ready to impale them if they should lose their balance. 'Quit it,' she said sharply. 'Don't you dare to maul me just because I daren't wiggle.' "

In some short-stories by Clem Yore there is rich humor unmistakably of the cattle-country, and cowboys' conversation just enough of a jargon not to seem a trick of the author's trade.

There is a scene in his *Easy Goin' of the Box Plumb Bob,* when a cowboy arrives at a ranch:

"As they rolled into the ranch-yard Splittin' Bill rushed out to meet the wagon and caught sight of the slender figure beside Jerkin'.

"'Rootin' Tootin', look w'at this yere old locoed Santa Claus brung us,' he yelled back at the bunkhouse. Jerkin' don't give a damn what rides with him.'

"'Hallo, y'old horned toad,' cried Easy Goin', leaping from his seat. 'How y'u all lives so long is one of the seven wondehs of the universe. Touch my flesh, y'u old son-of-a-gun.'

"'Darn my gizzard,' yelled Spittin' Bill, grasping his hand, 'if y'u aint arrived just in time. Boy, y'u is uglier'n hell still, ain't y'u? How c'n a man live with a face like that?"

Such horseplay is not a shade deeper than the genuine; it is the friendly humor of the cattle-country. But in the same story is a paragraph explaining the affection of the ranch-owner's daughter for the cowboy: "Superb mistress of her own mind as she was, Mazie found this retiring quality in Easy Goin' a thing of charm. She allowed no occasion to arise which would imbue him with thoughts of her femininity. Yet, all the while, he was essential to her; a great and growing love for his society was coming to flower within her."

The conflict between the hackneyed philosophy with its effusively bad grammar, and the careless badinage of the meeting of old friends, is the pathos of the Western-story magazine—the submerging of such faithful characterizations as may appear, in a welter of bad psychology and threadbare situations.

"*Cowboy Magazine,* New York City.

GENTLEMEN: I have been an ardent reader of your magazine for about a year and wish to state it's the best buy out for 20 cents."

"All I know of the West is what I read, but I feel like I belong there, that's how *Cowboy Magazine* stories impress me. I am a lover of books, and since I am reading your stories my passion for books has doubled."

"So let the hunter shoot his game,
Give the movie fan his screen,
The radiolite his XYZ,
Let other folks do what they please,
Just leave this treasure trove for me—
My Cowboy Magazine."

So there seems some justification for the literary maltreatment of the cowboy. There are audiences. . . .

CHAPTER FOURTEEN

THE MOVING-PICTURE COWBOY

IN 1869 Ned Buntline came to Omaha, his coat glittering with the medals he had collected; naturally he attracted attention. A certain army officer took pleasure in being seen with the renowned Buntline, and in the course of conversation told of Bill Cody, Army scout at Fort McPherson, three hundred miles west. Buntline scented "copy;" he made the journey, and a few days after his arrival Buffalo Bill returned from a campaign against the Indians. The scout gave the writer the many flamboyant details of his life, and Buntline, a new hero discovered, went back to New York to embroider the already spectacular narrative.

There followed, besides the *New York Mercury* articles and paper-bound panegyrics, a drama, "Buffalo Bill, the King of the Border Men," which played successfully in New York.

Cody came to New York in 1873, in time to see the play; Buntline had arranged, of course, that Cody be "recognized," and the "King of the Border Men," in person, was called before the curtain.

The applause that greeted Cody's curtain speech probably gave Buntline the idea of bringing the West to the stage. In a conference with friends at "Sandy Spencer's place" (once famed for its good cheer) Buntline secured financial backing.

On a Wednesday morning a few months later Buntline met Cody at Chicago. The buffalo-hunter had brought with him Texas Jack and Wild Bill Hickok, two frontiersmen of reputation. Half an hour after the meeting, Buntline rented the Chicago Amphitheatre for the following week. Then he organized himself into a company, and went to lunch. Cody and Wild Bill were to hire some "Indians" from the Chicago streets, and Buntline was to write the play. "The Scout of the Plains" was completed that same evening. (A novel written at Baldpate of the Seven Keys took four times as long, and was probably no better.) Buffalo Bill was the adventurous hero; Texas Jack and Wild Bill were to jump on the stage just in the nick of time to sever the rope which bound Buffalo Bill to the burning stake, and shout, "Now come on, you Redskins!" Then the three frontiersmen were to shoot the forlorn Indians until each had died several times and the audience was choking with the smoke.

"The Scout of the Plains" was a success, although the dramatic critics offered humbly dissenting opinions; and Buffalo Bill was now firmly established as a professional hero. The play triumphantly toured the East; and no city was more delighted than Boston.

Cody's own entertainment, the famous Wild West show, was organized in 1880, and continued to play, with occasional interruptions, until Cody's death. The program in 1910, when the show was enlarged into the Buffalo Bill Wild West—Pawnee Bill Far East Great Combination, as it is remembered, included:

A Grand Review.
The World's Rough Riders, introduced and led by Buffalo Bill.
U. S. Artillery and Cavalry Drill.
The Buffalo and the Famous Huntsman in pursuit of his native game.
The Prairie, under a scorching sun—"Oh, what a good drink! Pass it around."
Mexican Joe illustrating the use of a lasso.
Perfection of High-School Equestrianism.

Mr. Rhoda Royal's Famed Blue Ribbon Thoroughbreds.
Rossi's Musical Elephants.
Riding Wild Bucking Horses and Mules, introducing the only lady bucking horse rider in the world.
Buffalo Bill shooting glass balls.
Football on Horseback, between Indians and Cowboys.
The Final Salute! Buffalo Bill Bids You Good-by.

Somewhere in this sensational entertainment the Deadwood coach was brought forward; the Indians attacked it, the passengers screamed, and Buffalo Bill and his faithful cowboys rode to the rescue and the Indians bit the dust again.

How were the millions of youngsters that hailed Buffalo Bill as a greater man than Mr. Barnum to know that cowboys very infrequently matched themselves against Indians for a rollicking game of football? The Buffalo Bill Wild West Show was not a hilarious succession of anachronisms to them; it was the West, it was history. And when the moving pictures came to these same millions of youngsters, only a little grown-up, it did not matter if Indians clad in six-inch aprons shot clouds of arrows at cowboys hugging rifles salvaged from the Spanish-American War—if in another moment a troop of Government cavalrymen in neat dun breeches sallied over a hillcrest and charged the Indian hordes. The Final Salute of Buffalo Bill had been a benediction; and his illustrated sermon was never to be forgotten.

In a tableau that signalized the passing of the magic-lantern, the end of parlor entertainment and the development of movie palaces, Buffalo Bill was unconsciously the chief actor. One Mr. Goldenberg, in 1910, presented a series of slide pictures of the Buffalo Bill—Pawnee Bill Great Combination. There were twenty-five slides, all colored, nearly all representing Buffalo Bill, taming bucking bronchos, shooting Indians, pursuing his native game. . . . But in the same year Mr. Powers made moving pictures of the Wild West Show, "three hundred thrills in three hundred reels." Mr. Goldenberg was left, like Galsworthy's cabman, to mourn the passing order; the three reels of cowboys and Indians and horses and buffaloes made "movie history" for 1910, and Mr. Powers was started on the road to riches.

Every Saturday of this same year, and for several years after, the Essanay Company released a one-reel "Broncho Billy" story; it might be called "Broncho Billy and the New Schoolma'am," "Broncho Billy and the Navajo Maid," "Broncho Billy Begins Life Anew". . . . Week after week the same cowboy with the crooked nose and the likeable grin loved and rode and fought. The characters he played were always noble types, even when the part was that of a highwayman; he might change his loves each succeeding Saturday, but he always retained his virile purity. To impressionable critics his rugged face suggested the rock-bound coast the Puritans trod; his smile and the light in his eyes, when the moon comes out in its glory. In the summer of 1913 newspapers gravely printed the story of a certain little Dorothy who suffered from pneumonia; Dorothy, "peaked and anemic, the shadow of herself," was condemned to a second operation. The child resisted desperately, until her mother cried, inspired, "Remember Broncho Billy! You know Broncho Billy is brave and never breaks his word." And Dorothy sweetly submitted.

But there were many Western movies besides these every-Saturday miracle-plays; so many that it seemed in these early years that a great purpose of the moving picture was the tracing of the Western epic. Real cowboys were used in these movies; all outdoors offered itself for scenery. As the weeks passed, as "The Toll of the Desert," "The Taming of Texas Pete," "The Cowboy's Old Mother," "The Vengeance of the Range," and hundreds of others were issued, applauded, and forgotten, the screen epic of the West took shape. The chapter of that epic which may be called "The Cowboy and the Rustler's Daughter" may be summarized thus:

The cattle rustler is saved from his just fate by his pretty daughter who gallops up, severs the rope at a shot, holds the avenging cowboys at bay with her pistol and covers the retreat of her father. In sheer admiration at her pluck the boys permit him to escape. The scenes showing the grazing cattle, the stealing of the herd, the running fight between the rustler and the cowboys, follow in quick succession, overflowing with snappy action. It ends with a pretty love scene in which the girl faints after the crisis is past, and Bob, a dashing cowboy, tenderly revives her, wins her hand and makes plans for future happiness.

The cinema has fashioned in black-and-white; *Pilgrim's Progress* becomes graphic realism, and cowboys must be very, very good or monstrously wicked. Sam Bass, a typical villain if the short-lived, individualistic cow-country may be said to produce types, is passed over, and Billy the Kid, the killer, humorless, despicable, becomes the ideal Western villain. Sam Bass led his men into Fort Worth, bought each of them a horse and a flashy, stylish cowboy outfit, bought drinks for the crowd in the best saloons of the town; when Jackson had brought his wounded chief from Round Rock into the woods, and declared that he would stay and fight off the rangers, "No, Frank," said Bass, "I'm done for. You go ahead." Sam Bass was too human, too subtle a blend of good and bad. Billy the Kid rode into Lincoln County, New Mexico, where John Chisum had driven his sixty thousand cattle with the jingle-bob brand into range that the smaller cattlemen could not hold against the invader; he had hired himself out as professional gunman to first one party, then the other, in the Lincoln County War. He "pumped lead" as a part of the day's business; in all, he killed at least twenty-one men, "not counting Indians and Mexicans." Billy the Kid was the ideal movie bandit; and the villains in the latest Zane Grey movies foot the long list of his imitators.

Nor has the cinema admitted that the cowboy was a workman, with an unmodern devotion to his world—the range, its cattle, its horses, his fellow-cowboys. Of the several hundred cowboys who wrote little sketches of themselves in *The Trail Drivers of Texas,* most never married; very few married before they became full-fledged ranchmen. The glistening silk shirts, the deftly-carved wristlets, the *conchos* and kid gloves, that brand a Western "star" as surely as his immaculate cheeks, are graces added by a later age. The cowboys' wristlets were usually made from the skirt of an old saddle; a shirt that glittered in the sunlight was an abomination; and no cowboy who cared for his chances of survival ever went into a gun-fight with his gloves on.

The screen-epic of the West developed its curiosities innocently and unintentionally. Many were borrowed from literature; many were the improvisations of directors who had graduated from back-stage in musical comedies and provincial stock companies.

Since the days of set "programs" of short pictures, when movie-palace managers contracted at a stroke for a thousand or more photoplays and producers manufactured the films with the same largess, the stories have been bought from the Western magazines or written by a studio hack who had usually once been a contributor to cowboy-story magazines. Within the last few years, following the vogue of James Oliver Curwood's stories of the Northwest, the stories of Zane Grey have set the fashion for Western movies. If women would not patronize Western movies, good box-office logic suggested the bringing of femininity into the Western movies. The Zane Grey stories have delighted matinée audiences in "best houses" hitherto closed to Western films. Now Babylonian episodes and allegorical interludes may not be unexpected in the "upper-class" Western photoplay. In a recent Tom Mix movie that genial, genuine cowboy found himself thrust suddenly (by way of a dream) into the Middle Ages, with Ann Pennington frolicking atop the manorial dinner-table! The more common Western movies, made for the fifteen-cent theaters, continue to stress gunplay, fast riding—in a word, "action." These movies, designed for the most remote tenth of the fifty million Americans who patronize the movies weekly, may not proceed at the leisurely trot of a stallion leading his mares to water, but only—always—with the headlong dash of that stallion when men are pursuing with ropes and guns.

There have been many, many cowboys in Western movies, but seldom has there been evidence of a director who knew the West. James Cruze, in directing Emerson Hough's "North of 36," worked with a leading man who had but lately graduated from playing dress-suited villains in photoplays of "high society," and a delicately-coiffured leading lady who brought into each scene suggestions of a Connecticut riding academy—yet by virtue of the excellence of his material and his own intelligence Mr. Cruze made "North of 36" a first-rate photoplay. Earl Hudson, producing "Sundown" from his own story, apparently written hastily to take advantage of a drive of several thousand cattle from one state to another—no common occurrence since 1900—created truly and sympathetically; "Sundown" is undoubtedly the best of all Western photoplays.

The "star system," multiplied since the days of Broncho Billy, has worked well for the Western movies. William S. Hart, successfully surviving his work in "The Virginian" on the legitmate stage, acting, with a desperate earnestness and often in a mood more Indian than Pioneer; Ed Gibson, Westerner, stunt rider in rodeos, a cowboy in every gesture; Harry Carey; Tom Mix—these actors have been consistently identified with the better-than-average Western movie. Late reports put Tom Mix's salary at two-thirds of a million a year; reads a newspaper despatch, "Tom Mix has bought a home site in Beverly Hills. He will erect upon the property a Spanish mansion costing a quarter of a million. There will be nine marble bathrooms and a butler in a powdered wig and knee pants. The beautifully landscaped grounds will be dotted with a swimming pool, tennis courts and art garages, but no corrals." Such is the reward of one who has brought the flavor of Western romance to the fifty millions.

But these men can only bring interesting, honest personalities to the material that others give them. And one of the latest cinema enterprises is the weaving of a serial photoplay, "with great attention paid to historical authenticity of the West," about the sensational articles, "The Great West That Was," signed by Buffalo Bill. So the legend of the swashbuckling Westerner, half hero, half mountebank, is carried on.

CHAPTER FIFTEEN

THE ARISTOCRACY OF NOVELISTS

EVERY orthodox Western novel, sooner or later, finds its way into the seventy-five cent shelves of bookstores, department stores, drug stores, from the Atlantic to California. Well bound, fairly well printed, encased in gorgeous jackets of several colors, they make a pretty display. The shelves are ever changing; they are cultural media for half a nation, and they offer new titles on new jackets as endlessly, as monotonously, as the Western-story magazines appear.

But from a short story of several thousand words dashed off to be printed in one of the magazines for those who "just read," to a book, permanent in appearance at least, noticed pleasantly by some ever-obliging literary critics, is a wide gap: length has brought responsibility, dignity has brought care. Many of the seventy-five cent Western novels offer surprising entertainment—cleverly sketched characters, a neat situation or two, journalistic accuracy, the whole dose as pleasant as it is innocuous. A novel by Max Brand, for instance, is much better than a short-story by Max Brand.

Perhaps the improvement is largely because women are interested in the seventy-five cent fiction. A magazine with a garish cover depicting a red-shirted cowboy spinning his lariat toward a bull about to overtake a young lady, the lariat directed at the bull or at the lady according to the month of issue, may not very well be displayed in the street-car; but a book may. And the feminine taste that has certainly brought a well-grooved smoothness and a quiet flippancy into the typical American short-story may also have brought those qualities into the typical Western novel. One of the most popular books of the cow-country ever written was *The Little Knight of the X Bar B,* by Mary K. Maule. She had only a vague idea of the range country: "Between, away to the north and west as far as the eye could see, ran the great cactus-strewn, sage-covered prairies; here brown, here grey, here green; here touched with a myriad shifting, changing, opaline colors; now level as a floor, now rolling; now dipping down to tiny, wandering streams—the great plains of Wyoming and Montana—the great cattle-country of the Northwest." Of cowboys she reveals less; she speaks of the "comical and picturesque cowboys," of "the rude men, already removing their boots and clothing with a view to turning in." But she had once conducted a vice crusade for the *New York American;* honeyed moralities dripped readily from her pen, and the book went into edition after edition. Support from girls and women who turned for the moment from Eleanor Gates and Gene Stratton-Porter alone could have sustained it.

But in the procession of range-country novels that bloom and fade on the seventy-five-cent shelves, four names have seemed fixed. B. M. Bower, William McLeod Raine, Charles Alden Seltzer, Clarence Edward Mulford—these four, a constellation, are the aristocrats of cow-country fiction; though writing of familiar things, each has become a personality that readers have recognized and appreciated. Over them all in popularity is Zane Grey, who has touched several times on the cattle-country in his hurried scrivening of a gigantic Epic of the West. Harold Bell Wright has twice written of the cattle-country.

In one of Wright's novels a stranger, "footing it," meets one Joe Conley, cowboy, leading a horse through a corral gate. Joe, "dropping the saddle and blanket on the ground, approached his horse's head. Immediately the animal sprang back, with head high and eyes defiant; but there was no escape, for the rawhide riata was still securely held by his master. There was a short, sharp scuffle that sent the gravel by the roadside flying—the controlling bit was between the reluctant teeth—and the cowboy, who had silently taken the horse's objection as a matter of course, adjusted the blanket, and with the easy skill of long practice swung the heavy saddle to its place. As the cowboy caught the dangling cinch, and with a deft hand tucked the latigo strap through the ring and drew it tight, there was a look of almost pathetic wistfulness on the watching stranger's face—a look of wistfulness and admiration and envy."

The stranger, if you like, is Wright—liking the cowboy and admiring his skill, but wistful, because one who had been a preacher could not fully understand the careless gusto of this cowboy in the corral.

Wright has ridden the ranges and worked in the roundups; his descriptions of the "land of wide mesas, of wild, rolling pastures and broad untilled valley meadows" in *When a Man's a*

Man and *The Son of His Father* are products of this experience. He has used the cow-country as a background, but as a background it has been well used.

The best of the cattle-country fiction that the "bargain bookshelves" have known, setting aside *North of 36,* have been *West Is West,* by Eugene Manlove Rhodes, and *The Ridin' Kid from Powder River,* by Henry Herbert Knibbs. Both these "literary novelists" are of the range; one, Rhodes, was himself a cowboy for twenty-five years. Knibbs has written cow-boy songs that the cowboys have made a part of their own folk-lore. "Riders of the Stars"—

Give us a range and our horses and ropes, open the pearly gate,
And turn us loose in the unfenced blue riding the sunset rounds,
Hunting each stray in the Milky Way and running the rancho straight,
Not crowding the dogie stars too much on their way to the bedding grounds—

was better known to the cowboy-camps than many a song that the first Texas cowboys brought up the trail with them.

The Ridin' Kid from Powder River follows the fortunes of Young Pete, the Ridin' Kid—as real a cowboy as Owen Wister's Lin McLean, not at all the traditional cowboy hero (I quote Knibbs) "whose deadly accuracy, lightning-like swiftness, appalling freedom from accident, ostrich-like stomach and camel-like ability to go without water, earn him the plaudits of a legion of admiring readers." *West is West* is the story of a range war, the working out of the code: "It's not the custom to war without fresh offense, openly given. You must not smile and shoot. You must not shoot an unarmed man, and you must not shoot an unwarned man. . . . The rattlesnake's code, to warn before he strikes, no better: a queer, lop-sided, topsy-turvy, jumbled and senseless code—but a code for all that."

The most cuddled, the most admired, of all the cowboy heroes has been Chip of the Flying U.

When B. M. Bower (Bertha M. Sinclair) first invented Chip, in 1906, she herself was not sure of him: he was shadowy in outline; he quoted Shakespeare, Scott, and Burns by the page; he was a woman-hater; and he was a philosopher—"Sometimes even of late years, when he stood guard over the cattle at night, and got to thinking—oh, it was hell to be all alone in the world!" In appearance he was just like any other young cowboy hero: "His face was thin, and refined, and strong—the strength of level brows, straight nose and square chin, with a pair of paradoxical lips, which were curved and womanish in their sensitiveness; the refinement was an intangible expression which belonged to no particular feature but pervaded the whole face." But as this first novel, *Chip of the Flying U,* developed, Chip grew; he became human, likable, actually a cowboy.

The plot of the novel is familiar to many who have never read *Chip*—the story of the ranchman's sister who comes out West to spend the summer, of the supposedly woman-proof cowboy who is sent to meet her at the station, of the love that arises between them, of petty tiffs (true love never runs smooth), of the cowboy's fall from a horse, of his awakening from a month of the girl's nursing to a new and greater happiness. . . . Sometimes it is the niece of the ranchman, rather than his sister, who comes out for a summer's visit; and sometimes it is the foreman, not one of the regular cowboys, who wins her heart. But in *Chip,* as in many a novel, the minor characters are its salvation; the cowboys of the Flying U, if their creator does call them "The Happy Family," are a hard-playing, hard-working, convincing outfit.

In *The Flying U Ranch* "The Happy Family" comes into its own; Chip is married, promoted, practically disposed of; and the outfit seems now to belong to the range, not by any chance to Hollywood. The novel starts with the coming of an Irish-Spanish cowpuncher, immaculate and aloof, into the outfit. The cowboys resent this egotist in their midst, and "initiate" him in disagreeable ways, finally dressing his Angora chaps with a curling-iron; but when they learn of his invading Mexico and winning a bull-riding contest, they relent, and the Irish-Spanish cowboy is made one of the "Family." The novel moves forward with the outfit for its hero, into a story of the altercations between cowboys and sheepmen—a faithful story that the range itself might have seen. Of Slim, one of the oldest cowboys of the outfit, the author says, "He had worked for the Flying U when it was strictly a bachelor outfit, and with the tenacity of slow minds he held J. G. Whitmore, his beloved 'Old Man,' as but a degree lower than that mysterious power which made the sun to shine"; and with the Flying U outfit bound in clannish loyalty to their boss, the sheepmen are made black villains. By this contrast the author avoids meeting squarely the issue between sheepmen and cattlemen, and the novel ends happily when the villains are dispersed and the sheep are sold.

A better, truer book was the next, *The Flying U's Last Stand.* The era of barbed wire has come; but "The Happy Family" is retained on the Flying U pay roll, "just as if they were actually needed." "Cowpunchers to the bone though they were, they bent backs over irrigating ditches, and sweated in hayfields, just for the sake of staying together on the ranch." The tale is of a "Land Syndicate" for locating nesters on Government land—land greatly overrated and misrepresented, for the profit of the Syndicate. To forestall the graft and save the land for the Flying U, the cowboys decide to "homestead" the country for themselves, and save it for the cattle-country it was meant to be. The pitifully unequipped homesteaders that the Syndicate advertising has caught from the cities, the legal complications of settling a homestead, the revolt of the cowboys as this new generation comes with its hoes and its barbed wire to break up the open range into little private pens—Mrs. Sinclair has written of it well, only to break the faith near the close of the novel for a kidnaping and the defection of one of the "Happy Family" for the love of a nester girl.

Mrs. Sinclair's *Range Dwellers* is the story of a young rounder sent by his father to a Montana ranch to get a clean start. The young tenderfoot makes good, and wins by his dashing impudence the daughter of his father's old enemy, a neighbor ranchman—a moving-picture plot that of course found its way to the movies.

With William MacLeod Raine the psychoanalysed heroine comes into Western fiction. To take one girl of several, the heroine of *Oh, You Tex!* (one of those novels about the love of a foreman for the ranchman's daughter) was "Slim and lissome, the dew of childhood was on her lips, and the mist of it was in her eyes. But when she slanted her eyes toward Arthur Ridley, it was not the child that peeped shyly and eagerly from out beneath them. Her heart was answering the world-old call of youth to youth." And again, as she thinks of the hero, "In her soft, liquid eyes lurked the hunger for sex adventure." Hardly Freudian analysis, of course; rather of the school of those books from Mudie's circulating library that Raine may have known when he was a youngster in his native England. But his plot, his people, are distinctively American—such as his good-bad villain, Homer Dinsmore, unmistakably: "His hand had been against every man's, but at least he had fought fair and been loyal to his pals. And there had never been a good woman afraid to look him in the face."

A typical Raine novel is *Wyoming.*

"From a wonderful blue sky poured down upon the land a bath of sunbeat. The air was like wine, pure and strong, and above the desert swam the pure, untempered light of Wyoming." And here Helen, the heroine, newly a ranchowner, finds the cattle-country more or less terrified by one Bannister, who herds sheep in a cattleman's country.

A case of confused identities is soon revealed; the threads separate to reveal Bannister, leader of a gang of cut-throats, and his cousin, the sheepman—one of the galaxy of range-country heroes of whom it has been written, "No young Greek god's head could have risen more superbly above the brick-tanned column of the neck than this close-cropped curly one." Helen is worthy of him; as one cowboy says, "When she turns that smile of hers loose on a fellow—well, there's sure sunshine in the air."

Helen is lost, found by the desperado, Bannister, and taken to his cabin. "Here was an adventure from the gods— a stubborn will to break, the pride of a haughty beauty to trail in the dust, her untamed heart to break if need be. The lust of battle was upon him." And he hisses—almost exactly as a hero of Rex Beach's had hissed before—"What I want I get one way or another, and don't y'u forget it, my girl." And he hisses further: "Y'u'll crawl on your knees to me and beg pardon before I'm through with y'u, my beauty." But because the vanity of the man demanded a surrender of the spirit as well as a surrender of the flesh, conflict is delayed, and Helen's virtue is preserved until a rescue is effected.

When the desperado's right-hand man is shot, the sheepman Bannister realizes that neither he nor the girl will be safe until the gang is wiped out; and the shooting begins.

"He held her close, knew the sweet delight of contact with the supple, surrendered figure, then released her as she drew away in maidenly reserve." But the maidenly reserve was only momentary, to permit of final explanations; and the novel is ended.

In *Mavericks* the sheepman-cattleman feud is a hazy background for another attempt of a handsome egotist to bend a girl to his will. *Brand Blotters* treats again of the war between sheepmen and cattlemen—here faithfully, carefully, calmly, as the background of the love story of one who "looked out of cool, gray eyes upon a man's world that had often put him to the acid test" and a girl whose standards were those of the West, who could love only one "who would go the limit."

Charles Alden Seltzer writes grimly of grim, steel-like men; a Seltzer novel may almost be known by its number of men that die with their boots on. When this humorless intensity of his writing is fitted to his subject, when his hero is logically a thin-lipped, hard-eyed gunfighter with a single-track mind, his novels are successful. The best is probably *The Boss of the Lazy Y,* with his protagonist "a slumbering volcano of passion that might at any time become active and destroying," one who muses, "What influence had made him a hardened, embittered, merciless demon of a man whose passions threatened always to wash away the dam of his self-control?" Bound if he wishes to come into his inheritance to the control of a woman as dogged and unyielding as himself, he gradually softens into the kind of man she can love; but to the world he is still a "merciless demon," and in the time of his regeneration he shoots to kill. In *The Range Boss* the girl loathes the man she loves because of his killings, which she, with her Eastern code, cannot forgive; but the author happily overrides the difficulty by having the lady herself shoot a man—a villain about to ravish her.

Clarence Edward Mulford found a stock character in Hop-a-long Cassidy and a stock setting in the Bar-20 Ranch; both have served him well more than once. Hop-a-long rises nobly to sinister circumstances, and dominates easily in humorous byplay; through a welter of conventional situations he has preserved an individuality that assures his popularity with those who like their heroes chivalrous but don't object to a little gunplay.

Have only dramatic critics the grace and honesty to damn a work ("Abie's Irish Rose" comes to mind) that the public takes enthusiastically into its list of things worth while—and chuckle while they damn? It is no longer good form to burn incense to Harold Bell Wright; but about the literary abilities of Zane Grey there is a discreet silence, except for innumerable semi-apologetic tributes to his "well-known descriptive powers." For the critics, it seems, Grey is

A man whom few there are to love,
And none who dare to shoot.

Zane Grey, D.D.S. (Pennsylvania, 1896), with years of dental accomplishment in New York to his credit, turned gentleman of letters in 1904; and by 1921, when he wrote his remarkable preface for *To the Last Man,* he had come to conclude, in unconscious mimicry of Owen Wister, that the public will always recognize—and buy—a good book, if only it is good enough, and has a broad appeal. The broad appeal of Zane Grey is the romantic West.

"My long labors," he writes, "have been devoted to making stories resemble the times they depict. I have loved the West for its vastness, its contrast, its beauty and color and life, for its wildness and violence, and for the fact that I have seen how it developed great men and women who died unknown and unsung." But his romances, as he calls them, are the grim, gory conflicts of Sadists who are also supermen, women who are hypersexual yet strangely virginal. Stewart, his typical hero, is "a combination of fire, strength, and action. There was something vital and compelling in his presence." The superman again! But not as the Old Scout would have described him—Old Scout may have used pat, hackneyed phrases, but they had been forceful once.

When Ralph Cannon persuaded Grover Cleveland Alexander to comment on Willa Cather's *My Antonia,* he got more than he had bargained for. Said the great pitcher, "I much prefer Zane Grey's works. He puts a lot of zip into all of them. There's a fellow who has something on his fast one."

This "something," I believe, is legitimate explanation for his success; for interwoven with the appeal of a romance-laden West is practically every popular "appeal" that has enlivened the whole body of domestic fiction, from the glory of the Flag to the glory of woman's virginity, from a fiery democratic Americanism to the mystery of God-ordained love between man and woman, from the avenging strength of fighting men to the caveman tactics of lovers.

In *The Light of Western Stars* Alfred says to his sister Florence, "People called you the

American beauty, but you're more than that. You're the American girl! Majesty, marry no man unless you love him, and love an *American.* Stay away from Europe long enough to know the men—the real men of your own country." Grey describes the hero's love-tactics thus: "He had said straight out that he loved the girl—he had asked her to marry him—he kissed her—he hugged her—he lifted her upon his horse—he rode away with her through the night—and he married her. In whatever light Florence reviewed this thing she always came back to her first natural impression; it thrilled her, charmed her."

And in *To the Last Man,* an old burro-raiser says to Ellen, " 'Life is hard enough, God knows, but it's unfailin' true in the end to man or woman who finds the best in them an' stands by it' "—and again, " 'You are good—good as gold, Ellen, an' he knows it.' " And the hero did know it; by his own confession, "It was that—his strange faith in her purity—which had won her love." Of Ellen's love Grey writes, "The might of her passion was like the blaze of the sun. Before it all else retreated, diminished. . . . And love was like a burst from the depths of her, like a rushing spring of pure water, long underground, and at last propelled to the surface by a convulsion."

But the list, barely begun, becomes staggering. The whole effect is that of a brass band rushing without pause from *The Star-Spangled Banner* to *Dixie,* to *Yankee Doodle,* to *Silver Threads Among the Gold.*

These novelists of the seventy-five-cent shelves, engaged in the old game of "giving the public, not the intellectual but the ordinary, every-day public, what it wants, what it has always wanted, and always will want, the transitive, not the intransitive, verb of life—action, excitement, blood, a little love, a pepper of passion," have fallen into the pattern-evil. If some of these writers imitate others, the most successful of them imitate themselves. The niceties of structure in these tales are suspiciously like the niceties of structure in a five-reel photoplay; the novels are dreams made to order, and if the cowboy is only a lover he has played his part. These romances, though they may preserve a journalistic attention to broad detail, are not based in their characterizations and in their motives on the truth of human experience; and they are not true romances.

CHAPTER SIXTEEN

ANDY ADAMS

When "The Grand Canyon of the Colorado" was hung in the national capital, a critic wrote of Thomas Moran, the painter, "The art of such a man must, of necessity, be as health, as sincere and honest as the man himself. . . . I was more than ever convinced that the future of American art lies in being true to your own country."

For some Americans to be true to their own country in the fine sense that the art of Moran is true, they may celebrate the anniversary of the battle of San Jacinto, and keep perfectly sober on the Fourth of July; they need never have heard of Julia Ward Howe or Francis Scott Key, if they can sing:

Come all you Texas cowboys
And warning take from me,
And do not go to Montana
To spend your money free—

But stay at home in Texas
Where work lasts the year around,
And you will never catch consumption
By sleeping on the ground.

Andy Adams is such an American.

Andy Adams has little "cultural" background. His grammar has a barely commonplace accuracy. His sentences are sometimes hopelessly entangled, his phrases occasionally *clichages* that a hack-writer for the magazines might hesitate to use. He turned to fiction when he was past middle-age. No William Dean Howells had ever congratulated him on his literary pulse; no Henry James had ever spent a night blue-penciling a manuscript of his. But his first book, *The Log of a Cowboy,* is the finest piece of literature that the cattle-country has produced.

Fidelity in literature has always more than compensated for violations of academic technique. It is easy to point out that *Life on the Mississippi* is often rambling and diffuse, that *Moby Dick* is burdened with digression after digression and an allegory that is sometimes obtrusive; but it is not easy to show how much finer the work of Mark Twain and Hermann

Melville could have been if it had followed the patterns of William Gilmore Simms or Ethel Dell. *The Log of a Cowboy* cannot be graphed as a line of minor crux rising upon minor crux to catastrophe, thence descending in a graceful parabola to dénouement and conclusion; but it is the flesh on the skeleton that matters.

"My worst trouble was in getting away from home on the morning of starting. Mother and my sister, of course, shed a few tears; but my father, stern and unbending in his manner, gave me his benediction in these words: 'Thomas Moore, you're the third son to leave our roof, but your father's blessing goes with you. I left my own home for the sea before I was your age.' And as they all stood at the gate I climbed into my seat and rode away. . . ." And *The Log of a Cowboy* is fairly begun—the biography of a trail-herd in 1882, from Brownsville, in the southern point of Texas, to the Blackfoot agency near the northern border of Montana.

Under Jim Flood, straw-boss, the herd made the drive. "Priest told me this incident: Flood had hired a man at Red River the year before, when a self-appointed guardian present called Flood to one side and said, 'Don't you know that that man you've just hired is the worst drunkard in the country?'

"'No, I didn't know it,' replied Flood, 'but

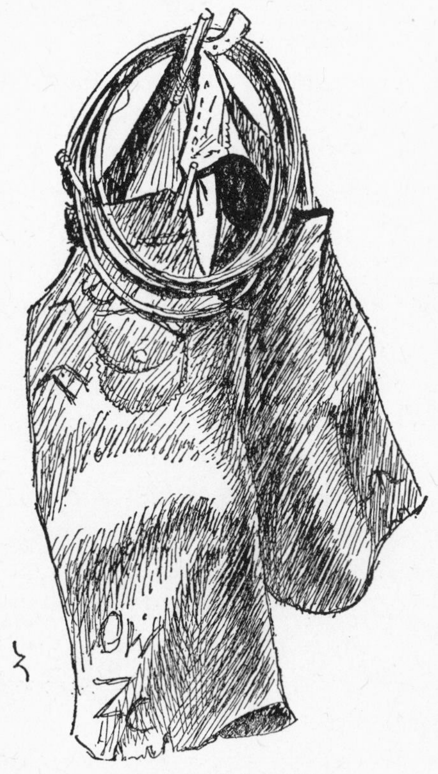

CHAPS AND ROPE

I'm glad to hear that he is. I don't want to ruin an innocent man, and a trail outfit is not supposed to have any morals. Just so the herd don't count out shy on the day of delivery, I don't mind how many drinks the outfit takes.'

"There was no driving to do; the cattle moved of their own free will as in ordinary travel." And the narrative itself seems to move of its own free will—leisurely, sure of itself, as natural as the trailmen themselves. For there are no grim, firm-lipped heroes among them, engrossed in their own humorless melodramas. Zane Grey would not know what to do with them.

As humanity comes back into literature, there will be more scenes with their people grouped about the dinner table. From the novels of Thomas Love Peacock to the tales of Andy Adams, except for some fugitive papers of Saintsbury's that weigh the merits of his wines and re-create the savors of halibut and whitefish, the delights of eating and of after-dinner talk have been ignored almost as much in literature as in life.

" Brother, dear, just think of those long slings with red cherries floating about in them that we'll be drinking, and picture us smoking cigars in a blaze. That thought alone ought to make a hard bed both soft and warm. . . ."

"McCann banked his fire, and the first guard, Wheat, Stallings, and Borrowstone, rode in from the herd, all singing an old chorus that had been composed, with little regard for music or sense, about a hotel they had stopped at the year before:

Sure it's one cent for coffee and two cents for
bread,
Three for a steak and five for a bed,
Sea breeze from the gutter wafts a salt water
smell
To the festive cowboy in the Southwestern
Hotel.

And again: "We all felt good, and McCann got up an extra spread for supper. We even had dried apples for dessert. McCann had talked the storekeeper at Doan's, where we got our last supper, out of some extras as a *pelon.* Among them was a can of jam. He sprung this on us as a surprise. Bob Blades toyed with the empty can in mingled admiration and disgust over a picture on the paper label. It was a supper scene, every figure wearing full dress. 'Now, that's General Grant,' said he, pointing with his finger, 'and this is Tom Ochiltree. I can't quite make out this other duck, but I reckon he's some big auger—a senator or governor, maybe. Them old girls have got their gall with them. That style of dress is what you call *lo* and *behold*. The whole passel ought to be ashamed. And they seem to be enjoying themselves, too.' "

Only an artist in living can introduce digressions like these into his writing. These are incidents told for their own sake, rich metal that needs no polishing. Wister would have literary work "reverently thorough"—"a writer can easily take himself too seriously, but he can never take his art too seriously." By never taking his art quite seriously, Andy Adams gave his fiction his refreshing freedom, and unlike Wister was never betrayed into fingering his necktie in public. "Once you get the ink on your fingers," reads a letter by Adams, "it is hard to quit. Fiction is the only field that pays—the human imagination is the source of all that is imperishable in literature." And that harmless little platitude is the nearest approach to stating a philosophy of his art, I believe, that Adams has made.

But Andy Adams was not a literary connoisseur out of the East, a *savant* in the novelist's art come West to swath his talent in "local color." He had come to Texas in 1882; in the next year he drove a herd of horses up the trail to Caldwell, Kansas. For five or six years afterwards he drove horse-herds into

Kansas; and near the end of the trail-days he turned to cattle-driving. Then Adams left the cattle-country, and followed the fast-disappearing frontier to Cripple Creek, Colorado, a mining camp "on the boom." He had the restlessness of the true frontiersman: "My heel seems to have itched, causing a wanderlust, from which I never fully recovered—at least, still a vagabond."

When *The Log of a Cowboy* appeared the reading public already "knew what it wanted" in its cowboy stories; from the sensational paper-backs and Owen Wister (*The Virginian* was still "the most talked-about novel" when Andy Adam's first book appeared) the cowboy had been enveloped in an aura of romantic virtue, with a tinge of manly wickedness to intensify his charm and make him worth marrying to reform. Andy Adams was too true to be good; and since, in his own words, he "could never . . . use a fifth wheel"—since he could not weave into his stories a girl, to be thrown into the arms of his cowboy-hero for a rousing finish, Adams was catalogued by most of those who noticed *The Log of a Cowboy* as one of those colloquial fellows who somehow slip into the publisher's lists, inconspicuous in the midst of a group of novelists who really understood their craft.

But there followed other novels by Andy Adams—all published by a Boston firm, the books of Andy Adams probably their only item in the far-flung field of Western fiction. The novels sold, after a fashion; if there had been more bookstores west of the Mississippi, more would have been sold.

Never a herd-owner himself, Adams has in *The Outlet* and *Reed Anthony, Cowman*, and in his one essay at juvenile fiction, *Wells Brothers, the Young Cattle Kings,* identified himself with the catlemen rather than with the cowboy. *The Outlet*—just now back in print, after several years when it could only be found in out-of-the-way bookstores—is the leisurely narrative of a single drive, much like *The Log of a Cowboy* in its bare outline, but with the interest sharply shifted to financial problems—delivery on time, counter-claims of a clever group of criminals, and legal actions. *Reed Anthony, Cowman,* is the story of a cattleman's successes and failures—mostly successes—through the seasons. Perhaps because *The Log of a Cowboy* is concerned very little with profit and loss, and is much more concerned with the dignity and the excitement of the spectacle of the drive and with the work and the ways of the men who drove, it is a better book than *The Outlet* or *Reed Anthony, Cowman.*

A Texas Matchmaker, the only book by Adams that does not deal with the trail, is a story of a Texas ranch of the early days; Adams dallies with romance and wedlock, quietly amused at his own theme, writing with twinkling, unobtrusive humor and digressing often for deft fillips of cowboy repartee—a style peculiar to Adams among Western-story writers, as many fine qualities are peculiar to Adams among Western-story writers.

Cattle Brands is Adams' one volume of short stories. Reflecting the secret assurance of the cowboys that the range-country was the best in the world, Adams sublimely disregards plot, as though implying that a yarn needs no structure to be interesting, if only it is a Western yarn.

A typical story is the first, *Drifting North.* "It was a wet, bad year on the Old Western Trail"; and a long overdue herd is waiting, waterbound. The owner of the herd, impatient, comes from Dodge City to the trail-camp, bringing with him a cattle-buyer. "Cowmen in those days prided themselves on their outfits, and Carter was a trifle gone on his men.

With the cattle on hand, drinking was out of the question, so the only way to show us any regard was to bring us a box of cigars. He must have brought those cigars from Texas, for they were wrapped in a copy of the Fort Worth *Gazette.* It was a month old and full of news. Every man in the outfit read and reread it. There were several train robberies reported in it, but that was common in those days. They had nominated for Governor The Little Cavalryman, Sol Ross, and this paper estimated that his majority would be at least two hundred thousand. We were all anxious to get home in time to vote for him. . . .

"That night around camp the smoke was curling upward from those cigars in clouds. When supper was over and the guards arranged for the night, story-telling was in order." The cattle-buyer tells of three bank-robbers who were caught and hanged; one of the cowboys tells of Mexican guides who betrayed their employers; the boss, Carter, gives the story of his flight once to avoid a bandit; and the foreman Baughman—"he had learned to take things as they came, play the cards as they fell, and not fret himself about little things that could not be helped"—tells of a holdup that he witnessed in the Colorado mining-country. Then—"It was an ideal night. Millions of stars flecked the sky overhead. No one seemed willing to sleep. We had heard the evening gun and the trumpets sounding tattoo over at the fort, but their warnings of the closing day were not for us. The guards changed, the cattle sleeping like babes in a trundle-bed." And the story is over. What matters the wet, bad year—the flood holding back the herd—the deal of the boss and the cattle-buyer—Sol Ross running for Governor down in Texas? Adams is willing to drop these threads, and close his story with the smoldering of the night's campfire. And the reader is as well satisfied as is Adams.

For a few years the readers of the Western-story magazines had known "Will James" as a name signed in the corner of pen-sketches that caught the play of muscles of man and beast, the glint of horseflesh, the friendly wrinkles of a cowpuncher's face, better than any sketches had caught these things since Russell's—when, about 1923, there began to appear in the bulkiest and most prosperous literary weekly in America stories of cowboy customs, casual descriptions of the old range ways, flavored strongly with a likable, happy-go-lucky personality that seemed strangely out-of-place in a magazine world of stock salesmen, personality-plus executives, and imperious princesses in *décolleté.*

About Christmas of 1924 these stories appeared in a book, *Cowboys North and South,* that must have pleased lovers of good printing and good binding, as it delighted lovers of folk-literature. Like some cowboy-ballads, these stories seemed the experiences of a whole group filtered through the personality of one man. "I was born and raised in the cow country, I am a cowboy, and what's put down in these pages is . . . what I've lived, seen, and went thru before I ever had any idea that my writing and sketches would ever appear before the public," James declares in his preface; but no one would have raised the issue. The art of re-creating a psychology has not yet reached that fine point where any one not a cowboy could have written these yarns. The passing of the Longhorn, the sectional differences in cowboy customs, the work of the winter months on a cattle ranch (no one who has seen it will ever forget that sketch of a cow standing guard over her cold-numbed calf as a black bear lunges forward), the coming of the nesters—this is the stuff of which James writes, and writes in a new way.

James has lately turned to short stories. With the thinness of his plots and his attempts at popular humor his dialect seems superficial and affected, his attitude precious. The difference has been in the loss of his personality—an open, honest personality that needs the capital *I* for its approach and fact for its material.

"To my way of thinking," writes Will James, "anybody with a lot of nerve is never real bad all the way, whether he be a horse thief, or cattle rustler—the excitement he gets out of it is what he likes most, and you can bet your boots that even tho' he may be dealing from the bottom of the deck, he's taking his from those that won't suffer from the loss, or maybe even miss it; you're plumb safe when that kind rides up to your camp to leave your silver mounted spurs and bits scattered around as usual, and most likely if he sees you're in need of a fresh horse he'll be real liberal in offering you the pick of his string—only danger is, if you're caught riding one of them ponies, it may be kind of hard to explain just how you come in possession of said animal."

If Andy Adams is the optimist of cowboy literature, Will James is its sentimentalist. In *Cowboys North and South* James brought sentimentality into the Western scene without also bringing in ranchmen's nieces and homesteaders' daughters. The fragrance of his writing is thoroughly masculine; it is the aroma of a mellowed pipe.

There is an open, obvious conflict between the cowboy literature of Andy Adams, Emerson Hough, of Eugene Manlove Rhodes and Henry Herbert Knibbs, Will James with his short-stories and Charles A. Siringo with his autobiographies—and the fiction of the Western-story magazines and the "bargain bookshelf" novelists. The tendency of this pattern-fiction of the news-stands is to simplify the cowboy-era and blur the cowboy himself into a hazy mythology, with pasteboard figures moving through typewriter-created sagas, a marital desuetude the unchanging goal. The tendency of the writings of Andy Adams and the others I have named with him is to preserve the cowboy and the range in the clarity of history; and the historical picture can never be so complete that it will explain away the wonder and the mystery of the West.

Already a sweet sentimental haze is overlying the great spectacle of the range, the long trail from the heart of Texas to the cow-towns of Kansas, and beyond to the edge of the moun-

"Hoo-de-i-yea-e-ho, travel you Doe-gies
Hoo-de-i-yea-e-ho, travel along—
Hoo-de-i-yea-e-ho, step to it cattle,
For old Wyoming will be your new home!"

OLD TEXAS TRAIL HERD SONG.

tains of Montana; the drive to Kansas is becoming confused with the caravan to Cathay, and in a twilight of romanticism the lowing of cattle and the clatter of the *caballado* is wafted back in the same breeze with the tinkling of the camels bells and the evening song of the bulbul. Each year the old trail-drivers of Texas gather in convention, and in the irresistible aroma of pipes that have long been smoked and long been loved they review their trail-driving days; and each year a smaller number returns to this "roundup" to talk and smoke. Their Association is planning now a monument to the old trail-drivers. When their grandsons stand before the statue and feel the breath of the stone upon them, they will see old Sir Kay in new clothes, or they will see Young Jim, the Pecos Kid. The issue rests largely with the impression their own cowboy literature offers them. It is a choice of platitudes or of personalities.

BIBLIOGRAPHY

THE COWBOY [1]

ADAMS, ANDY. *Cattle Brands* (Houghton Mifflin, 1906).

——— *The Log of a Cowboy* (Houghton Mifflin, 1903).

——— *Reed Anthony, Cowman* (Houghton Mifflin, 1907).

——— "Western Interpreters." *Southwest Review*, X (October, 1924).

ALDRIDGE, REGINALD. *Ranch Notes in Kansas, etc.* (London, 1884).

AMBULO, JOHN. "Cattle on a Thousand Hills." *Overland Monthly*, n.s. IX (March, 1887).

BAKER, RAY STANNARD. "The Tragedy of the Range." *Century Magazine*, LXIV (August, 1902).

BARKER, ROBERT M. "On a Western Ranch." *Fortnightly Review*, XLVII (April 1, 1887).

BARROW, F. H. "The Passing West." *Overland Monthly*, n.s. LV (June, 1910).

BAUMANN, JOHN. "Experiences of a Cowboy." *Lippincott's Monthly*, XXXVIII (September, 1886).

BECHDOLT, FREDERICK R. *Tales of the Old-Timers.* (Century, New York, 1924).

[1] The publisher is given only for volumes published within the past twenty years.

——— *When the West Was Young.* (Century, New York, 1922).

Black, Z. E. "America's Unhorsed Knight and His Lady." *Sunset, XXXV* (December, 1915).

Brisbin, General James S., *The Beef Bonanza; or, How to Get Rich on the Plains.* (Philadelphia, 1881).

Bronson, Edgar Beecher. *Cowboy Life on the Western Plains.* (Grosset and Dunlap, New York, 1910).

——— *The Red Blooded Heroes of the Frontier.* (Grosset and Dunlap, New York, 1910).

Buckman, George R. "Ranches and Rancheros of the Far West." *Lippincott's Monthly,* XXIX (May, 1882).

Burns, Walter Noble. *The Saga of Billy the Kid.* (Doubleday, Page, New York, 1926).

Burton, George Lee. "With the Colorado Punchers on a Roundup." *Outing,* XXXVI (May, 1900).

Chapman, Arthur. "The Cowboy of Today." *World's Work,* VIII (September, 1904).

——— "The Cowboy War." *Outing,* LVIII (July, 1911).

——— "The Johnson County Cattle War." *The Frontier,* I (March, 1925).

——— "The Men Who Tamed the Cow-Towns." *Outing,* XLV (November, 1904).

Clay, John. *My Life on the Range.* (Privately printed, 1924).

Cook, James H. "Driving Texas Long-Horn Cattle Through Nebraska." *Nebraska State Historical Society Proceedings,* XVIII.

——— *Fifty Years on the Old Frontier.* (Yale University Press, New Haven, 1923).

COOLIDGE, DANE. "The Passing of the Cowboy." *Sunset*, XVI (January, 1906).

——— "With the Cherrycow Outfit." *Sunset*, XXIV (May, 1910).

COWAN, JOHN L. "Knights and Barons of Our Western Empire." *Overland Monthly*, n.s. XLVIII (October, 1906).

"Cowboy Life," *Outing*, XIX (December, 1891; January, February, 1892).

"Cowboy's Finery." *Harper's Weekly*, LVII (January 11, 1913).

DALE, E. E. "History of the Ranch Cattle Industry in Oklahoma." *American Historical Association Report*, 1920.

DIMOCK, A. W. "A Real Wild West Show." *Harper's Weekly*, L (December 8, 1906).

DOBIE, J. FRANK. "The Chisholm Trail." *Country Gentleman* (February 28, 1925).

——— "Cowboy Songs." *Country Gentleman* (January 10, 1925).

——— "The Old Trail Drivers." *Country Gentleman* (February 14, 1925).

DRAPER, WILLIAM R. "Passing of the Texas Cowboy and the Big Ranches." *Overland Monthly*, n.s. XLV (February, 1905).

DUFFIELD, GEORGE C. "Driving Cattle from Texas to Iowa, 1866." *Annals of Iowa*, XIV (April, 1924).

FINGER, CHARLES J. *Sailor Chanties and Cowboy Songs.* (Haldeman-Julius Co., Girard, Kansas, 1923).

FRONTIER TIMES, J. Marvin Hunter, editor, Bandera, Texas. (A monthly magazine of frontier history.)

FURLONG, C. W. "Epic Drama of the West." *Harper's Monthly*, CXXXIII (August, 1916).

GROHMAN, W. BAILLE. "Cattle Ranches in the Far West." *Fortnightly Review*, XXXIV (October 1, 1880).

HARGER, CHARLES M. "Cattle Trails of the Prairies." *Scribner's*, XI (June, 1892).

HASTINGS, FRANK S. "A Ranchman's Recollections." (*The Breeder's Gazette*, Chicago, 1921).

HAYES, A. A. JR. *New Colorado and the Santa Fe Trail.* (New York, 1880).

HERRON, M. J. "The Passing of the Cowman." *Overland Monthly*, n.s. LV (February, 1910).

HILL, J. L. *The End of the Cattle Trail.* (J. L. Hill, Long Beach, Cal., 1923.)

HORNADAY, WILLIAM T. "Cowboys of the Northwest." *Cosmopolitan*, II (December, 1886).

HOUGH, EMERSON. *North of 36* (Appleton, 1923).

——— *The Story of the Cowboy* (Appleton, 1924, 1st ed. 1897).

HOWARD, R. R. "The Passing of the Cattle King." *Outlook*, XCVIII (May 27, 1911).

INNES, JOHN. "A Visit to a 'Round-up.'" *Canadian Magazine*, XVI (November, 1900).

JACQUES, MARY S. *Texan Ranch Life* (London, 1894).

JAMES, WILL. *Cowboys North and South* (Scribner's New York, 1924).

JAMES, W. S. *Cowboy Life in Texas; or, Twenty-seven Years a Maverick* (Chicago, n.d.).

LANIER, S. "The Texas Trail in the Seventies." *Outlook,* CV (November 15, 1913).

LARNED, WILLIAM T. "The Passing of the Cow-punchers." *Lippincott's Monthly,* LVI (August, 1895).

LIPP, G. A. "The Passing of the Western Cattle Ranches." *Overland Monthly,* n.s. LVI (February, 1914).

LOMAX, JOHN A. *Cowboy Songs and Other Frontier Ballads* (Macmillan, New York, several editions).

McCOY, JOSEPH G. *Historic Sketches of the Cattle Trade of the West and Southwest* (Kansas City, 1874).

McNEAL, T. A. *When Kansas Was Young* (Macmillan, New York, 1922).

MACKAY, MALCOLM S. *Cow Range and Hunting Trail* (Putnam's, 1925).

MAYO, EARL. "A Day's Work on a Cattle Ranch." *World's Work,* III (January, 1902).

METZGER, S. S. "A Day on the Ranch." *Sunset,* XXXVII (July, 1916).

NIMMO, JOSEPH, JR. "The American Cowboy." *Harper's Monthly,* CXXIII (November, 1886).

——— "The Range and Ranch Cattle Business in the United States." *House Ex. Doc.* 7, part iii, 2d Sess. 48th Cong.

NORTH, A. W. "Warfare on the Ranges." *Harper's Weekly,* LIII (July 10, 1909).

"Old-Time Cowboys Defend Emerson Hough." *Literary Digest International Book Review* (July, 1924).

PAINE, ALBERT BIGELOW. *Captain Bill McDonald, Texas Ranger* (J. B. Little and Ives, New York, 1909).

PAXSON, FREDERICK L. "The Cow Country." *American Historical Review,* XXII (October, 1916).

Pioneer Days in the Southwest from 1850 to 1879 (Guthrie, Okla., State Capital Co., 1919, (2d ed.).

POLLOCK, J. M. *The Unvarnished West; Ranching as I Found It* (London, n.d.).

POST, CHARLES C. *Ten Years a Cowboy* (Chicago, 1899).

Prose and Poetry of the Live Stock Industry of the United States, vol. 1 (no others published). Denver and Kansas City, 1905.

REMINGTON, FREDERIC. *Crooked Trails* (New York, (1898).

——— "In the Sierra Nevada with the Punchers." *Harper's Monthly,* LXXXVIII (February, 1894).

ROBERTS, MORLEY. *The Western Avernus* (London, 1904 "new ed.").

ROLLINS, PHILIP ASHTON. *The Cowboy* (Scribner's, New York, 1922).

ROLT-WHEELER, FRANCIS. *The Book of Cowboys* (Lothrop, Lee and Shepard, Boston, 1921).

ROOSEVELT, THEODORE. *Hunting Trips of a Ranchman* (New York, 1885).

——— "In Cowboy Land." *Outlook,* CIV (May 24, 1913).

——— *Ranch Life and the Hunting Trail* (New York, 1888).

SANTEE, ROSS. "The Payson Rodeo." *Century,* CIV (May, 1922).

SHELDON, A. E. "A Nebraska Episode of the Wyoming Cattle War." *Nebraska State Historical Society Proceedings,* V, (2d series).

SHEPHERD, MAJOR W. *Prairie Experiences in Handling Cattle and Sheep* (London, 1884).

SIRINGO, CHARLES A. *A Lone Star Cowboy* (Santa Fe, 1919).

——— *A Texas Cowboy; or, Fifteen Years on the Hurricane Deck of a Spanish Pony* (Chicago and New York, 1886).

SLIGH, J. E. "The Lincoln County War." *Overland Monthly,* n.s. LII (August, 1908).

THOMAS, A. R. "On a Powder River Ranch." *Overland Monthly,* n.s. LVIII (October, 1911).

THORP, N. H. *Songs of the Cowboys.* (Houghton Mifflin, n. d.)

The Trail Drivers of Texas (2 vols.), San Antonio, Texas, The Old Time Trail Drivers' Historical Association, 1922, 1923.

WHEELER, HOMER W. *The Frontier Trail; or, From Cowboy to Colonel* (Times-Mirror Press, Los Angeles, 1923).

WHITE, OWEN P. "The Brave and Untrue." *Colliers,* LXXVI (November 28, 1925).

WHITE, STEWART EDWARD. "On Cowboys." *Outlook,* LXXX (September 3, 1904).

WHITING, ELEANOR. "Five Days a Ranchwoman." *Outlook,* LXXXIII (August 25, 1906).

WILKESON, FRANK. "Cattle-Raising on the Plains." *Harper's Monthly,* LXXII (April, 1886).

Wister, Owen. "The Evolution of the Cow-Puncher." *Harper's Monthly*, XCI (September, 1895).

Zogbaum, Rufus F. "A Day's Drive with Montana Cowboys." *Harper's Monthly*, LXXI (July, 1885).

(1)

THE END